Introducing Microsoft System Center 2012 R2

Mitch Tulloch with Symon Perriman
and the System Center Team

PUBLISHED BY
Microsoft Press
A Division of Microsoft Corporation
One Microsoft Way
Redmond, Washington 98052-6399

Library of Congress Control Number: 2013949895
ISBN: 978-0-7356-8283-2

Microsoft Press books are available through booksellers and distributors worldwide. If you need support related to this book, email Microsoft Press Book Support at mspinput@microsoft.com. Please tell us what you think of this book at *http://www.microsoft.com/learning/booksurvey*.

Microsoft and the trademarks listed at *http://www.microsoft.com/about/legal/en/us/IntellectualProperty/ Trademarks/EN-US.aspx* are trademarks of the Microsoft group of companies. All other marks are property of their respective owners.

The example companies, organizations, products, domain names, email addresses, logos, people, places, and events depicted herein are fictitious. No association with any real company, organization, product, domain name, email address, logo, person, place, or event is intended or should be inferred.

This book expresses the author's views and opinions. The information contained in this book is provided without any express, statutory, or implied warranties. Neither the authors, Microsoft Corporation, nor its resellers, or distributors will be held liable for any damages caused or alleged to be caused either directly or indirectly by this book.

Acquisitions Editor: Anne Hamilton
Developmental Editor: Karen Szall
Project Editors: Carol Dillingham and Valerie Woolley
Editorial Production: Christian Holdener, S4Carlisle Publishing Services
Copyeditor: Roger LeBlanc
Indexer: Jean Skipp

Contents

What do you think of this book? We want to hear from you!

Microsoft is interested in hearing your feedback so we can continually improve our
books and learning resources for you. To participate in a brief online survey, please visit:

microsoft.com/learning/booksurvey

Chapter 10 Windows Azure Pack   127

What do you think of this book? We want to hear from you!

Microsoft is interested in hearing your feedback so we can continually improve our
books and learning resources for you. To participate in a brief online survey, please visit:

microsoft.com/learning/booksurvey

Foreword

It is an exciting time to be in IT, as we are on the frontier of yet another major evolution in the datacenter. With the explosive growth of server virtualization, we have seen the benefits of hardware consolidation, higher-availability and mobility, improved application compatibility, simplified deployment and management, and multitenancy, all of which have led to reduced operating costs. Many enterprises are just starting their journey to the next phase, the private cloud, which through the virtualization of networking and storage is simplifying resource pooling and allocation. Self-service and automation capabilities are freeing up time for the IT staff by eliminating repetitive tasks and allowing them to focus on adding more value to the business through new and improved service offerings. Now Microsoft is leading the industry in the next phase of this evolution with Windows Server 2012 R2, System Center 2012 R2 and Windows Azure—the transition to the hybrid cloud.

The hybrid cloud provides a datacenter without boundaries, allowing IT to take advantage of both on-premises resources and third-party hosting providers, as well as the public cloud using Windows Azure. Services should be able to run on any of these three clouds while providing an identical end-user experience. However, this consistency across clouds needs to happen for everyone involved in the lifecycle of these enterprise applications, and Microsoft is uniquely positioned to provide these capabilities to all consumers of IT services.

Now developers can use Visual Studio and Team Foundation Server to code applications that run on and between these clouds. Database administrators can use SQL Server and SQL Azure to consistently analyze and manage data from any cloud. Security experts can use Active Directory to secure and federate their users across clouds and from any device. Last, but certainly not least, IT professionals can create Hyper-V virtual machines and unify the management of their datacenter resources and applications using System Center.

Microsoft's strength in this space comes from almost two decades of experience running cloud services, starting with MSN Hotmail in 1997, and today offering the broadest cloud portfolio in the world, with over 200 distributed services. These include Xbox Live with 40+ million gamers, Office Web Apps with 50+ millions users, Outlook.com with 60+ million accounts, SkyDrive with 200+ million users, and Skype with 280+ millions users, not to mention the billions of objects managed daily by Bing, Exchange Hosted Services, and Windows Azure. It is from this experience that Microsoft has learned how to efficiently configure and manage cloud services on any scale, and we've incorporated the best practices we've identified into the tools we provide our customers in Windows Server and System Center.

Throughout this book, you will see the latest enhancements from System Center 2012 R2 to provide the most advanced and integrated datacenter management tools throughout the stack, supporting diverse hardware, hypervisors, operating systems, applications and clouds, and allowing you to lead your company toward the datacenter of the future. We hope you are ready to take this journey with us!

Symon Perriman, Senior Technical Evangelist, Microsoft Corporation

Introduction

Microsoft System Center is one of the three pillars of Microsoft's Cloud OS vision that will transform the traditional datacenter environment, help businesses unlock insights in data stored anywhere, enable the development of a wide range of modern business applications, and empower IT to support users who work anywhere while being able to manage any device in a secure and consistent way. The other two pillars of the Cloud OS are, of course, Windows Server 2012 R2 and Windows Azure, and Microsoft Press has recently released free Introducing books on these platforms as well.

Whether you are new to System Center or are already using it in your business, this book has something that should interest you. The capabilities of each component of System Center 2012 R2 are first described and then demonstrated chapter by chapter. Real-world and under-the-hood insights are also provided by insiders at Microsoft who live and breathe System Center, and those of you who are experienced with the platform will benefit from the wisdom and experience of these experts. We also included a list of additional resources at the end of each chapter where you can learn more about each System Center component.

Acknowledgments

Three groups of people have helped make this book possible, and as authors we'd like to thank them all here.

First, the following experts at Microsoft have contributed sidebars that explain and demonstrate some of the powerful and exciting capabilities in System Center 2012 R2:

- Chris Samson
- David Apolinar
- Heath Lawson
- John McCabe
- John Savill
- Marton Csiki
- Mike Gaal
- MS Anand
- Nick Rosenfeld
- Rob Davies

Second, the following Microsoft insiders have peer-reviewed the content of this book to help us ensure it's as accurate as possible:

- Anshuman Nangia
- John Ballard
- Justin Incarnato
- Laura Cruz
- Michael Kelley
- Martin Booth
- Matt Galbraith
- Richard Rundle
- Won Huh
- Wally Mead

Finally, we'd also like to thank Carol Dillingham, Content Project Manager at Microsoft Press; Christian Holdener at S4Carlisle Publishing Services; and copyeditor Roger LeBlanc.

Errata & book support

We've made every effort to ensure the accuracy of this content and its companion content. Any errors that have been reported since this content was published are listed at:

http://aka.ms/IntroSysCentR2/errata

If you find an error that is not already listed, you can report it to us through the same page.

If you need additional support, email Microsoft Press Book Support at *mspinput@microsoft.com*.

Please note that product support for Microsoft software is not offered through the addresses above.

We want to hear from you

At Microsoft Press, your satisfaction is our top priority, and your feedback our most valuable asset. Please tell us what you think of this book at:

http://aka.ms/tellpress

The survey is short, and we read every one of your comments and ideas. Thanks in advance for your input!

Stay in touch

Let's keep the conversation going! We're on Twitter: *http://twitter.com/ MicrosoftPress*.

Cloud computing

Modernizing the datacenter to the cloud era is at the heart of what business today is thinking about, and System Center 2012 R2 is a key part of Microsoft's solution for achieving such a transformation. The chapter in this part examines Microsoft's vision, called the *Cloud OS*, and how System Center can help make this vision a reality for your business.

CHAPTER 1

System Center and the Cloud OS

This chapter provides a brief overview of Microsoft's Cloud OS vision and how Microsoft System Center can make this vision a reality for customers. The topics covered in this chapter include

- Microsoft's Cloud OS vision
- From vision to reality
- How to learn more

Microsoft's Cloud OS vision

While the focus of this book is on System Center 2012 R2, it's important that we begin by stepping back to get the big picture of how System Center fits into Microsoft's overall vision for how the datacenter can be transformed today to be cloud-ready.

Why the Cloud OS?

Things are changing more rapidly than ever for us in enterprise IT today. We need new tools for automating datacenter provisioning, management, and monitoring. We need these tools to be able to manage both physical and virtual workloads on-premises and across public and service-provider clouds. We also need tools for automating tasks and workflows both in the datacenter and in the cloud. These tools need to be scalable, flexible, and secure.

In addition to managing desktop and laptop computers, we now have to manage diverse mobile devices like tablets and smartphones. And they're frequently personal devices owned by the users themselves, making it tougher to standardize due to the variety of platforms. Our existing technologies need to be integrated with new platforms that allow device registration and enrollment, policy-based management, and management from the cloud. And we need to be able to deliver a secure and personalized experience on any device, anywhere, at any time.

We also have to deal with the apps users run on mobile devices. Deploying and managing these apps present us with new challenges to accelerate the application life cycle, the handoff from developer to infrastructure specialists, also known as "DevOps." And we have to deal with greater amounts of data than ever before. Big data needs powerful new tools for business intelligence to unlock the value of data stored both on-premises and in the cloud using Microsoft SQL Server. In fact, System Center is built on top of SQL Server and uses it as the database for all the System Center components. Although almost all System Center components could share a single SQL Server instance, it is recommended to run each component on its own host or as an individual virtual machine, along with its own SQL Server instance.

And we need to accomplish all this without breaking our ever-constrained IT budgets. Fortunately, the licensing model for System Center 2012 (R2) has been significantly simplified Now every System Center component comes with the single license, so there is no longer a need to pick which component you want the most based on a budget limitation—you get them all! Additionally, the System Center license also includes the SQL Server licenses that are required for the databases. This new model will accelerate your transition to a cloud-ready platform because you will be provided with all the tools you need for infrastructure provisioning and management, automation, self-service, IT service management, and application management. Now you can start to roll out all these new systems at your own pace, without worrying about licensing restrictions or limitations.

What is the Cloud OS?

The term *Cloud OS* represents Microsoft's visionary approach to how IT can deliver on all these needs and challenges businesses are facing today. The Cloud OS vision embraces datacenters, private clouds, public clouds, and hybrid solutions. Three key platforms comprise the Cloud OS:

- **Windows Server 2012 R2**   Provides the foundation for building enterprise-class datacenter and hybrid cloud solutions that are simple to deploy, cost-effective, application-focused, and user-centric.

- **System Center 2012 R2**   Delivers a unified management experience across on-premises, service provider, and Windows Azure environments, in a manner that's simple, cost-effective, application-focused, and enterprise-class.

- **Windows Azure**   Provides an open and flexible cloud platform for building, deploying, and managing applications using almost any language, tool, or framework and running them in a secure public cloud hosted in a global network of Microsoft-managed datacenters. Windows Azure also lets you integrate your public cloud applications with your existing on-premises IT environment to enable hybrid-cloud capabilities.

Whether it's more devices, more apps, or more data your business is facing, Microsoft's three Cloud OS platforms and the technologies that integrate with them can help deliver the scale, speed, and agility you need while protecting your existing investments.

What can the Cloud OS do for you?

Microsoft's Cloud OS vision has four key goals:

- **Transform the datacenter**   Windows Server and System Center can manage the compute, storage, and networking resources of the modern datacenter to support its virtual machines, applications, and services. Together, they can transform this environment to make it capable of handling rapidly changing needs and unexpected opportunities while providing continuous service availability. System Center and Windows Azure can extend the datacenter beyond its traditional boundaries into the cloud to leverage economies of scale and keep IT costs under control. New automation platforms and tools are provided so that IT can deliver applications and services dynamically on an as-needed basis.

- **Enable modern business applications**   Technology innovation is rapidly changing whole industries and business sectors today. These innovations in devices, data, and the cloud are creating a revolution in what applications can do and how people use them. System Center and Windows Azure provide tools for deploying, managing, and monitoring that can reach any device and extend to the cloud. Applications and data can be rapidly developed and provisioned both on-premises and in the cloud through improved efficiencies in the application-development life cycle.

- **Empower people-centric IT**   People today need to be able to do their jobs from virtually anywhere on any device so that they can stay productive. They expect and deserve a consistent experience across desktop computers, laptops, tablets, and smartphones. System Center provides a unified management experience for provisioning, managing, and monitoring end-user computers and mobile devices. Sensitive business data can be protected as it is accessed from these devices, especially when the device is owned by the user instead of the company.

- **Unlock insights on any data**   Business data is being generated faster and in greater quantities than ever before. System Center, Windows Azure, and SQL Server provide tools to be able to store, access, and analyze such data to find insights that can help grow business. Users can access data anywhere, at any time, on any device and use familiar and intuitive tools for business analytics and reporting.

From vision to reality

The primary focus of this book is on the first goal of Microsoft's Cloud OS vision: transforming the datacenter. System Center is key to turning this vision into a reality by providing the following customer benefits:

- **Datacenter without boundaries**   System Center helps keep management simple with a consistent experience across devices and platforms, including public, private, and service-provider clouds . It can scale up and scale down through easy access to cloud resources. And it can help increase the resiliency of services and applications with enterprise-grade offerings to balance needs across the business.

- **Cloud innovation everywhere** System Center helps reduce cost and increase flexibility through the simplified implementation of hybrid cloud models using a consistent toolset for developers (with Visual Studio), database admins (with SQL Server), security experts (with Active Directory), and IT professionals (with Hyper-V and System Center). It enables secure access to information and resources from any device, both on-premises and across clouds.

- **Dynamic application delivery** System Center lets you automate repetitive manual processes to reduce time and cost. You can manage and monitor systems, devices, and applications with enough detail to quickly fix problems when they occur through performance analysis at the code level. And it offers self-service options so that business units, departments, users, and customers can provision and manage applications and services both on-premises and in the cloud.

To help you understand how the Cloud OS vision can be transformed into a reality for your business, this book examines each of the components of System Center and how they can be used to transform your datacenter by implementing private cloud solutions.

The story begins in Part 2 with provisioning infrastructure. Chapter 2 examines how you can provision your infrastructure using System Center Virtual Machine Manager. Chapter 3 describes how System Center App Controller can be used to provide self-service capabilities for your virtual machines, services, and clouds while hiding the complexities of what takes place within the underlying infrastructure. Chapter 4 looks at configuring and securing your infrastructure using System Center Configuration Manager and System Center Endpoint Protection. And Chapter 5 discusses backup and recovery using System Center Data Protection Manager.

Part 3 continues the story with a look at how to implement two kinds of monitoring within your infrastructure. Chapter 6 covers real-time monitoring with System Center Operations Manager, while Chapter 7 examines proactive monitoring using System Center Advisor.

The story concludes in Part 4 with achieving your ultimate goal of building private clouds. Chapter 8 examines IT service management and self-service with System Center Service Manager, while Chapter 9 tells how to implement automation using System Center Orchestrator. Chapter 10 puts on the finishing touch by examining the Windows Azure Pack, which lets you run Windows Azure public-cloud technologies in your own datacenter with increased flexibility and control.

How to learn more

For more information about Microsoft's Cloud OS vision, see *http://aka.ms/cloud-os*.

For information about Windows Server, see *http://aka.ms/ws2012r2*.

For information about System Center, see *http://aka.ms/sc2012r2*.

For information about Windows Azure, see *http://aka.ms/windowsazure*.

For more information about System Center licensing, download the datasheet from *http://aka.ms/SCLicensing*.

Provisioning infrastructure

System Center 2012 R2 enables you to provision the physical and virtual infrastructure needed to build private cloud solutions both for enterprise datacenters and hosters. Built upon a foundation of Microsoft Windows Server 2012 R2 and extended into the public cloud through Windows Azure, such solutions can provide scalability and elasticity that can meet the needs of today's—and tomorrow's—businesses.

System Center 2012 R2 Virtual Machine Manager allows you to provision the virtualization hosts, host clusters, and infrastructure resources used to create and deploy virtual machines and services to private clouds. System Center 2012 R2 App Controller enables you to provision a self-service platform to allow end users to deploy and manage virtual machines and services in cloud environments. System Center 2012 R2 Configuration Manager provides you with a comprehensive solution for change and configuration management that enables you to provision operating systems, applications, software updates, and configuration to both servers and clients, whether physical or virtual. System Center 2012 R2 Data Protection Manager enables you to provide continuous data protection and recovery for servers, including the Hyper-V hosts on which your cloud solutions run, the virtual machines that host your business applications, and the Microsoft SQL Server databases that support all the System Center 2012 R2 roles.

This section of the book provides you with an introduction to Virtual Machine Manager, App Controller, Configuration Manager, and Data Protection Manager; examines these System Center components in action; provides expert insights from Microsoft insiders; and lists additional resources where you can learn more.

CHAPTER 2

Provisioning infrastructure with Virtual Machine Manager

This chapter provides a brief overview of System Center 2012 R2 Virtual Machine Manager. The topics covered in this chapter include

- Introduction to Virtual Machine Manager
- Virtual Machine Manager in action
- Insights from the experts
- How to learn more

Introduction to Virtual Machine Manager

Virtual Machine Manager (VMM) enables you to configure and manage the virtualization hosts, host clusters, and infrastructure resources used to create and deploy virtual machines (VMs) and services to private clouds. These infrastructure resources include host groups, networking resources, storage resources, and library servers and shares. Together these different resources constitute the *fabric* from which private clouds can be deployed and managed using the System Center family of products.

Hosts and host clusters

Virtual Machine Manager can manage multiple hypervisor platforms, including Microsoft Hyper-V hosts, Citrix XenServer hosts, and VMware ESX hosts. Virtual Machine Manager can also be used to manage Hyper-V, VMware, and Citrix host clusters to ensure the availability of virtual machines and services deployed on such hosts.

Host groups

To make it easier to manage large numbers of virtualization hosts and host clusters, Virtual Machine Manager lets you organize them into host groups. A *host group* is simply a logical grouping of virtualization hosts. Host groups can be created based on different criteria, such as the physical location of the hosts or how resources are allocated to them. By default, any host added to Virtual Machine Manager will initially be placed in the All Hosts host group.

Networking resources

Virtualization hosts, virtual machines, and services require networks in order to be able to communicate with each other, applications, and users. Virtual Machine Manager enables you to provision and manage a wide range of networking resources for the hosts and host clusters you use to build your private cloud. These different networking resources can include logical networks, which represent network sites defined by IP subnets, virtual local area networks (VLANs), or both; logical switches, which allow you to define a virtual network configuration as a template and apply it across Hyper-V hosts; static IP address pools and MAC address pools, which can be created for logical networks so that DHCP is not required; IP Address Management (IPAM), which allows you to display IP address utilization and inventory data; load balancers so that you can load-balance requests to virtual machines making up an application or service tier, along with a collection of Virtual IP Addresses (VIPs); and virtual switch extensions, which enable you to do such things as provide quality of service (QoS) or monitor network traffic.

Virtual Machine Manager also provides network virtualization capabilities, including support for creating and managing virtual networks and network gateways. Network virtualization is a parallel concept to a server virtualization, where it allows you to abstract and run multiple virtual networks on a single physical network. Network virtualization through VMM offers several advantages compared to using traditional networks. First it connects virtual machines to other virtual machines, hosts, or applications running on the same virtual network. When a VM gets moved to a different host, VMM will automatically migrate that virtual network with the VM so that it remains connected to the rest of the infrastructure. Network virtualization also allows multiple tenants to have their own isolated networks for security and privacy, as well as have their own IP address ranges for management flexibility. Finally, using a gateway, a VM running on a virtual network can connect to any physical network in the same site or a different location. System Center 2012 R2 Virtual Machine Manager even includes an inbox NVGRE gateway that can be deployed as a VM to provide this cross-network interoperability.

Storage resources

Virtualization hosts, virtual machines, and services require storage in order to store application data and settings and to access shared storage from multiple locations so that virtual machines can run on different hosts. Virtual Machine Manager enables you to discover, classify, provision, allocate, and assign both local storage, where the storage capacity is directly attached to the virtualization host, and remote storage, in which the task of storage management is offloaded from the host to an external storage device. In addition, Virtual Machine Manager supports both block storage—including Fibre Channel, iSCSI, and Serial

Attached SCSI (SAS) storage area networks (SANs)—and file storage using file shares that support the Server Message Block (SMB) 3.0 protocol. This last capability was first introduced in Virtual Machine Manager 2012 and enables you to use Virtual Machine Manager to create and manage Scale-out File Server (SoFS) instances running Windows Server 2012 to take advantage of such capabilities as storage pools and thin provisioning.

Library servers and shares

The Virtual Machine Manager library contains a catalog of resources used for creating and deploying virtual machines and services on virtualization hosts. These resources are of two types:

- **File-based resources** This type includes virtual hard disks, ISO images, Microsoft Windows PowerShell scripts, Microsoft SQL Server scripts, driver files, Microsoft Server Application Virtualization (Server App-V) packages, and answer files.
- **Non-file-based resources** This type includes virtual machine templates, service templates, and profiles used to standardize the creation of virtual machines and templates.

File-based resources are stored on the library servers themselves, while non-file-based resources are stored in the Virtual Machine Manager database. You can also add custom resources to the library—for example, a custom installation package or post-execution script.

Library resources are exposed for use through library shares. Each library server can have multiple shares. As your private cloud grows, you can scale out either by adding more library servers or more library shares as needed. You can also make your library servers and shares highly available by deploying the file server on a Windows Server Failover Cluster. In System Center 2012 R2, Virtual Machine Manager can now create, validate, and manage a file-server cluster.

Management server

The management server is the server on which the Virtual Machine Manager service runs. The management server controls communications with the Virtual Machine Manager database, library servers, and virtual machine hosts. Any commands issued through the Virtual Machine Manager console or using Windows PowerShell are processed by the management server. You can have multiple management consoles in an environment.

Day-to-day operations

Once you deploy Virtual Machine Manager in your environment, prepare your fabric by configuring host groups, networking and storage resources, and library servers and shares, and add virtualization hosts and other infrastructure servers (such as SoFS instances), you are ready to begin working with Virtual Machine Manager. Some of the day-to-day operations tasks you might perform include configuring self-service user roles, creating virtual machine templates, creating service templates, creating private clouds, deploying virtual machines to private clouds, deploying services to private clouds, scaling out services, managing fabric updates, monitoring the health of virtual machines, backing up the Virtual Machine Manager database, and so on.

Constructing the private cloud

Virtual Machine Manager is essential if you want to use the System Center platform to create and deploy a private cloud. The reason for this is because Virtual Machine Manager provides resource pooling, enables self-service, and supports the elasticity required to build cloud solutions. You can use Virtual Machine Manager to create a private cloud from a host group that contains any or all of the following types of hosts: Hyper-V, VMware ESX, and Citrix XenServer. You can also use Virtual Machine Manager to create a private cloud from a VMware resource pool if you have VMware vCenter Server deployed in your environment.

Although Virtual Machine Manager provides some basic building blocks for creating private clouds, you can build more robust cloud solutions by integrating Virtual Machine Manager with other System Center components, including the following:

- **Operations Manager** With Operations Manager, you can use the System Center Monitoring Pack for System Center 2012 Virtual Machine Manager to monitor the health of resources. It also provides reporting capabilities for your Virtual Machine Manager environment.

- **Orchestrator** Use Orchestrator to create workflows that interact with Virtual Machine Manager to automate common tasks.

- **Service Manager** This feature integrates with Virtual Machine Manager through the System Center Virtual Machine Manager Connector.

- **Data Protection Manager** Use this feature to back up your Hyper-V hosts, virtual machines, and applications running within virtual machines.

For more information on these System Center components, see their associated chapters in this book.

Virtual Machine Manager in action

Let's now look at a few examples of Virtual Machine Manager at work. Figure 2-1 shows the Virtual Machine Manager console with the VMs And Services workspace selected at the bottom left. This workspace is used to deploy and manage virtual machines, virtual networks, clouds, and tenants. In this screen shot, the administrator is reviewing the performance of the hosts to ensure that there is enough capacity to create a new virtual machine.

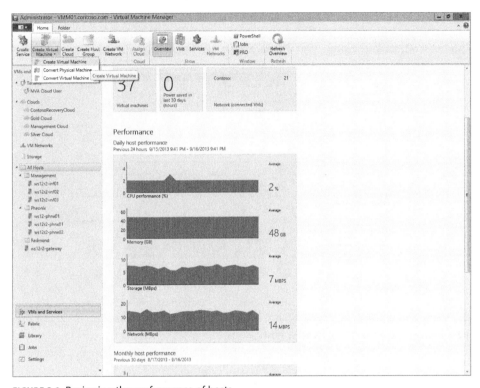

FIGURE 2-1 Reviewing the performance of hosts

Figure 2-2 shows the Virtual Machine Manager console with the Fabric workspace selected. This workspace is used to manage all the infrastructure servers, hosts, costs, networking, and storage components in your environment. In this screen shot, the administrator is reviewing the utilization and health of a Windows Server 2012 R2 Hyper-V host.

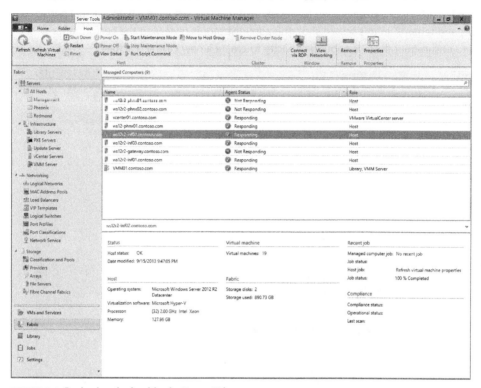

FIGURE 2-2 Reviewing the health of a Hyper-V host

Figure 2-3 again shows the Virtual Machine Manager console with the Fabric workspace selected. In this screen shot, the administrator is pooling the storage resources and creating tiers, which simplifies storage management and improves performance by taking advantage of the latest storage enhancements in Windows Server 2012 R2.

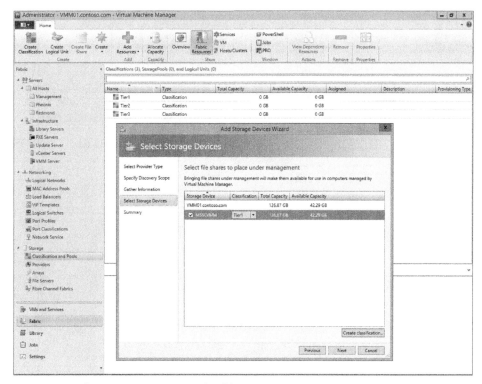

FIGURE 2-3 Pooling storage resources to simplify storage management

Figure 2-4 shows the Virtual Machine Manager console with the Fabric workspace selected once again. In this screen shot, the administrator has created a logical network to define the topology of the underlying physical networking infrastructure and is configuring the IP Address Pool settings for VMs that will deployed on this network.

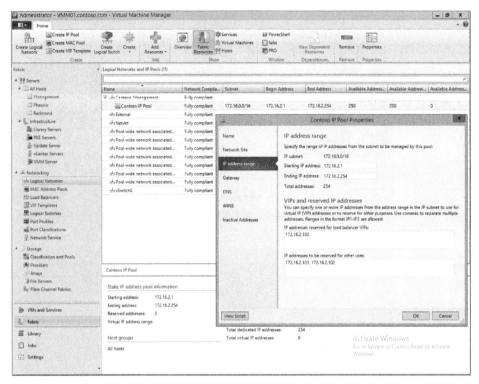

FIGURE 2-4 Configuring IP address pool settings for a logical network

Figure 2-5 shows the Virtual Machine Manager console with the Fabric workspace selected one more time. In this screen shot, the administrator is adding a new VMware vCenter Server to be placed under the management of Virtual Machine Manager. This addition will enable the administrator to use the VMware hosts just like Hyper-V hosts, allowing the ESX Servers to be added to the fabric and made available for VM placement.

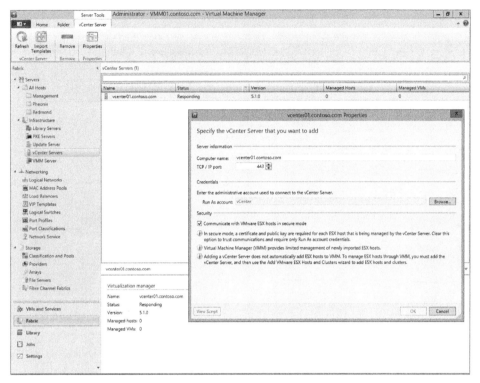

FIGURE 2-5 Adding a new VMware vCenter Server

Figure 2-6 shows the Virtual Machine Manager console with the Library workspace selected. This workspace is used to manage standardized resources that will be used by Virtual Machine Manager, such as Templates, Profiles, Self-Service Content, Library Servers, ISOs, virtual hard disks (VHDs), Software Update Catalogs, and more. In this screen shot, the administrator is reviewing a two-tier service template, which represents a distributed virtualized application running across both Hyper-V and Citrix XenServer hosts.

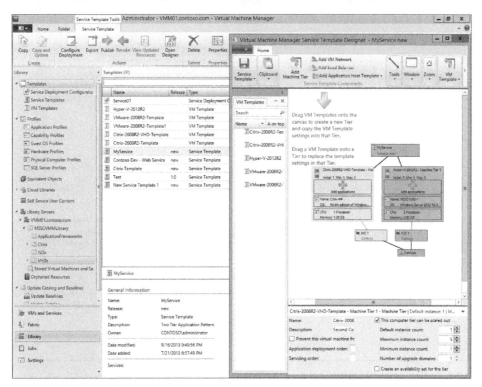

FIGURE 2-6 Example of a two-tier service template

Insights from the experts

We'll conclude this chapter by hearing from one of our experts at Microsoft about some new features that were added in this release of Virtual Machine Manager.

New functionality in Virtual Machine Manager 2012 R2

Virtual Machine Manager 2012 R2 adds some exciting new functionality and integration with Windows Server 2012 R2. The following sections highlight several of these new capabilities.

Integrating Virtual Machine Manager with IPAM

Virtual Machine Manager now extends address management to the IP Address Management (IPAM) feature of Windows Server 2012 R2 by leveraging a new network service in the Fabric manager as shown here:

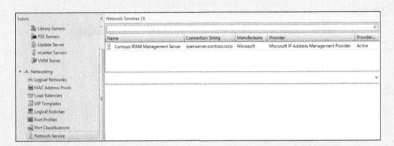

When Virtual Machine Manager is integrated with Windows Server 2012 R2 IPAM, the management of IP blocks within Virtual Machine Manager can be controlled through the IPAM user interface in Server Manager. This is particularly useful if another team is responsible for the network address spaces in the environment.

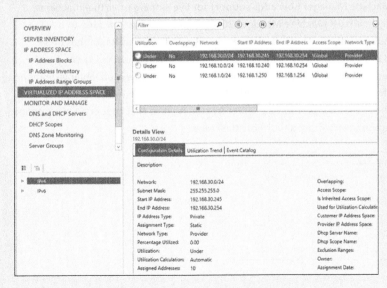

As an example of extended IPAM management, I'll show you how it is now possible to delete Virtual Machine Manager IP address pool blocks from the IPAM user interface in Server Manager. The network service in Virtual Machine Manager will refresh and reflect these changes:

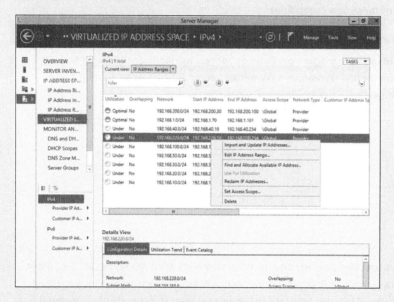

Live clone

Virtual Machine Manager now adds support for live cloning of virtual machines. Previously in Virtual Machine Manager 2012 SP1, for a virtual machine to be cloned, it first had to be powered off. As shown next, however, this limitation has been removed in Virtual Machine Manager 2012 R2, and the new capability can be of great use for copying production virtual machines into an isolated lab environment without having to shut down the production virtual machine. This could be used to troubleshoot a poorly performing server by cloning it so that the server stays online while the administrator troubleshoots the clone.

Online VHDX resize

Virtual Machine Manager now supports online resize of VHDX drives if the disk drives are attached to a SCSI adapter. Resizing includes both growing and shrinking the disks; however, resizing of VHD drives is not supported.

Support for differencing disks

Virtual Machine Manager now supports provisioning of virtual machines using differencing disks. This capability allows for ultrafast deployments of virtual machines because only a small child virtual machine needs to be created that points to the parent disk, rather than copying the full VHD for the operating system. The Hyper-V hosts can have a path defined for the caching of parent disks. This cached path can be a normal path or a shared SMB3 share:

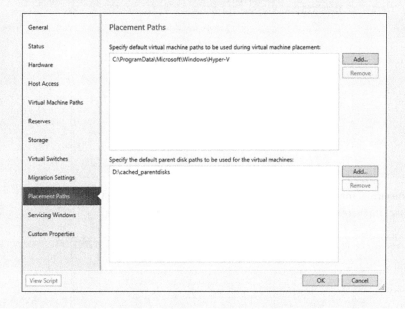

When deploying a virtual machine, you can now use differencing-disk optimizations for deployment. This capability uses the cached parent disk on the Hyper-V host:

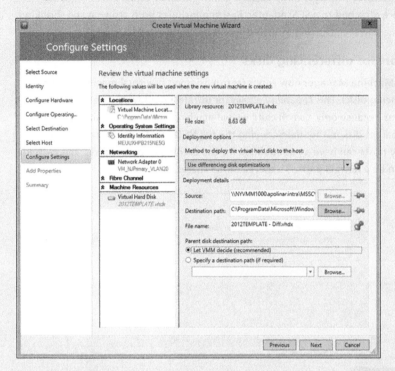

Once the virtual machine has been deployed, the properties of the virtual machine will reflect the parent disk as well as the differencing disk:

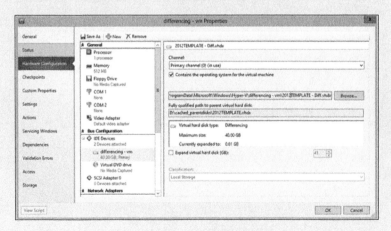

How to learn more

The following sections provide links to sites where you can learn more about Virtual Machine Manager.

Product home page

Your starting point for exploring, trying, buying, deploying, and supporting Virtual Machine Manager and other System Center 2012 R2 products is the System Center 2012 R2 home page on Microsoft's Server And Cloud Platform site at *http://www.microsoft.com/en-us/server-cloud/products/system-center-2012-r2/*.

TechNet Library

If you're already familiar with previous versions of Virtual Machine Manager, you might want to start with "What's New in VMM in System Center 2012 R2," found at *http://technet.microsoft.com/en-us/library/dn246490.aspx*. If you're new to Virtual Machine Manager, you can browse the full online documentation for Virtual Machine Manager starting from *http://technet.microsoft.com/en-us/library/gg610610.aspx*.

TechNet blogs

For the latest information about Virtual Machine Manager, follow the Virtual Machine Manager Engineering Blog at *http://blogs.technet.com/b/scvmm/*.

TechNet wiki

The Virtual Machine Manager wiki articles can be found at *http://social.technet.microsoft.com/wiki/contents/articles/705.wiki-virtualization-portal.aspx#System_Center_Virtual_Machine_Manager*.

TechNet forums

To get answers to your questions about Virtual Machine Manager, try posting to one of the Virtual Machine Manager forums on TechNet at *http://social.technet.microsoft.com/Forums/systemcenter/en-US/home?category=virtualmachinemanager*.

TechNet Evaluation Center

You can download evaluation versions of Virtual Machine Manager and other System Center 2012 R2 products from the TechNet Evaluation Center at *http://technet.microsoft.com/en-US/evalcenter/dn205295*.

TechNet Virtual Labs

You can try out Virtual Machine Manager and other System Center 2012 R2 products online using the TechNet Virtual Labs at *http://technet.microsoft.com/en-us/virtuallabs*.

Channel 9

Channel 9 on MSDN has lots of helpful videos on Virtual Machine Manager. See *http://channel9.msdn.com/search?term=VMM*.

Microsoft Virtual Academy

The Microsoft Virtual Academy has numerous online courses on Virtual Machine Manager and other System Center 2012 R2 products at *http://www.microsoftvirtualacademy.com/product-training/system-center*.

Twitter

@SystemCenter is your official Twitter source for System Center solutions and news. You can find reviews, discussions, and helpful information at *https://twitter.com/system_center*.

CHAPTER 3

Provisioning self-service with App Controller

This chapter provides a brief overview of System Center 2012 R2 App Controller. The topics covered in this chapter include

- Introduction to App Controller
- App Controller in action
- Insights from the experts
- How to learn more

Introduction to App Controller

App Controller provides a self-service experience for deploying and managing virtual machines (VMs) and services in cloud environments. The self-service experience provided by App Controller through a web browser is consistent across all types of clouds, including private, public, and hosted clouds. This capability makes App Controller the ideal platform for implementing the hybrid computing model.

Microsoft's approach to cloud computing involves two key platforms: System Center and Windows Azure. System Center enables enterprises to deploy and manage private clouds, which enables the enterprise to transition from a device-based infrastructure to a user-centric, service-based consumption model. Windows Azure is Microsoft's public cloud offering, and enterprises can use it to deploy and manage cloud solutions on a subscription basis. Additionally, you can use System Center to manage and monitor your virtual machine in third-party datacenters, allowing you to consume resources in service providers' clouds. App Controller can be thought of as the "glue" that ties these three clouds together, enabling the enterprise to build and manage private, service-provider, and public-cloud resources using a consistent management experience.

App Controller components

App Controller consists of one or more App Controller servers, a website hosted by Internet Information Services (IIS), a Microsoft SQL Server database, and a Microsoft Windows PowerShell module. This website can be accessed through any supported web browser, such as Internet Explorer.

The App Controller library is a logical representation of all library objects from clouds that have been registered in App Controller. These clouds can be private clouds associated with Virtual Machine Manager or the Windows Azure public cloud. The App Controller library can manage three kinds of shared storage: file shares on your network, private cloud libraries, and Windows Azure storage accounts.

Integration with Virtual Machine Manager

App Controller is tightly integrated with System Center 2012 R2 Virtual Machine Manager and is considered an extension of Virtual Machine Manager. In fact, one of the prerequisites for installing an App Controller server is that the Virtual Machine Manager console feature already be installed on the server. The version and service pack level of App Controller and Virtual Machine Manager must also match for them to work together.

Virtual Machine Manager 2012 and earlier included a Self Service Portal feature that could be deployed to allow users to provision virtual machines themselves based on the virtual machine templates available to the user. Beginning with Virtual Machine Manager 2012 SP1, however, the Self Service Portal feature was removed in favor of using the self-service capabilities provided by the web-based App Controller console.

Because App Controller relies on the role-based security model of Virtual Machine Manager, users of the App Controller console can see only the resources defined for the user role that has been assigned to them and perform only the tasks assigned to that role. Because administrators can use App Controller to delegate authority based on user roles, managing multitenant cloud environments can be greatly simplified by providing security at the user-role level rather than the individual member level.

Windows PowerShell support

App Controller includes a Windows PowerShell module that includes more than two dozen cmdlets. Any task you can perform using the App Controller console can also be performed using Windows PowerShell commands. This enables administrators to use Windows PowerShell to automate App Controller day-to-day operational tasks.

Day-to-day operations

Once App Controller has been installed and configured in your environment, you are ready to begin working with App Controller. Some of the day-to-day operations tasks you can perform include the following:

- Creating and managing user roles
- Delegating users
- Adding or removing library resources, such as file shares, private cloud libraries, and Windows Azure storage accounts
- Connecting to private or public clouds
- Copying files between file shares and private or public clouds
- Copying library resources between clouds of the same type
- Deploying virtual machine templates to private clouds
- Uploading virtual hard disks or images to Windows Azure
- Monitoring the usage of private and public clouds
- Backing up and restoring the App Controller database
- Performing any other cloud-related management tasks

App Controller in action

Let's now look at a few examples of App Controller at work. Figure 3-1 shows the Overview workspace of App Controller. This workspace shows the services and virtual machines running across any of the clouds, which include an on-premises private cloud, a Windows Azure cloud, and a cloud hosted by a service provider. In this screen shot, one of the virtual machines running in Windows Azure needs attention, and the self-service user is reviewing the recommendations from the Common Tasks and Online Help panes.

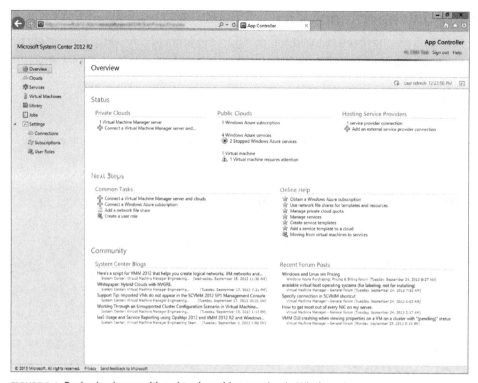

FIGURE 3-1 Reviewing issues with a virtual machine running in Windows Azure

Figure 3-2 shows the Services workspace of App Controller. This workspace is used to provide an overview of the Services (a collection of VMs) running in any of the clouds connected to App Controller. In this screen shot, a Service called Wiki0 is selected, which is running in a Production cloud on Windows Azure. The self-service user can see that the service is in West Europe and has two tiers, which are both healthy.

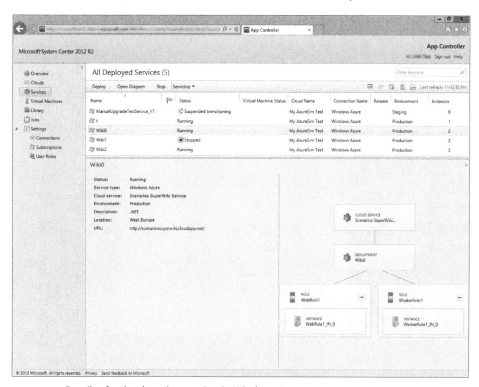

FIGURE 3-2 Details of a cloud service running in Windows Azure

Figure 3-3 shows the Library workspace of App Controller. This workspace is used to manage templates from Virtual Machine Manager, manage disks and images from Windows Azure, and also provide access to resources in other file shares. In this screen shot, the self-service user is reviewing the hardware configuration of a Windows Server 2012 R2 template hosted in the VMM Library.

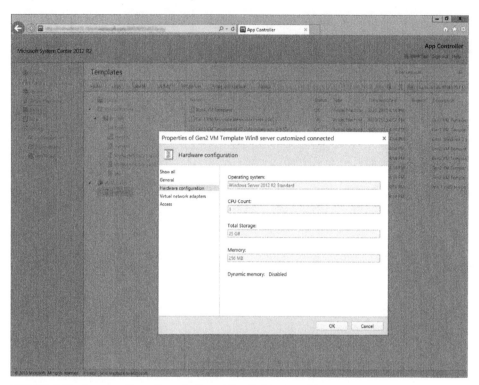

FIGURE 3-3 Hardware configuration of a Generation 2 virtual machine

Figure 3-4 shows the deployment of a new virtual machine to Windows Azure using App Controller. In this screen shot, a Windows Server 2012 VM is selected from a gallery of publicly available images, which also includes other Microsoft applications.

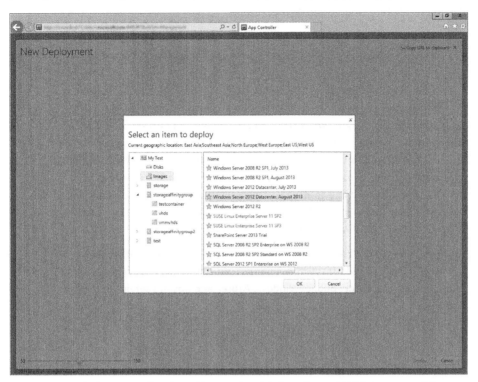

FIGURE 3-4 Deploying a new virtual machine running Windows Server 2012 Datacenter edition to Windows Azure

Insights from the experts

We'll conclude this chapter by hearing from one of our experts at Microsoft about how to set up and manage a hybrid cloud using App Controller.

Managing Hybrid clouds with System Center App Controller

As organizations progress with their journey to the cloud, transitioning from virtualized datacenters to private clouds, service-provider hosted clouds, and public clouds, we are seeing cloud administrators and business unit IT administrators of these organizations entrusted with managing these clouds. With each of these clouds on various virtualization platforms with different capabilities and different administrative consoles, administrators often find it difficult to manage them all, be it day-to-day tasks like provisioning, deprovisioning, start, stop, snapshot, or other tasks like migrating virtual machines between clouds (from a private cloud to the Windows Azure public cloud).

System Center 2012 R2 App Controller delivers a web interface that provides administrators and end users with a common self-service experience to manage resources across private, public (Windows Azure), and hosting service provider clouds:

Setting up clouds

App Controller connects to Virtual Machine Manager to provide private cloud management, and both App Controller and Virtual Machine Manager need to be running the same version (2012 or 2012 R2).

To connect to a service-provider cloud, the administrator enters the details provided by the hosting service provider, who will have configured System Center Provider Foundation with the tenant details and provided the necessary certificate to import into App Controller. Similarly, Windows Azure subscription details can be entered by providing the Subscription ID and Management certificate details.

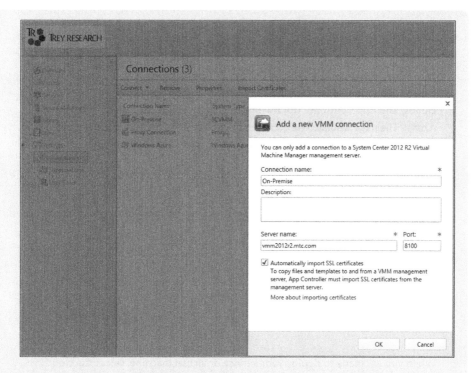

Access to hosting service-provider clouds and Windows Azure subscriptions can then be managed by creating or modifying the user role. The administrator can add users and groups from Active Directory that will have either read-only or full access to these clouds. In case there are multiple subscriptions, the administrator can choose which subscriptions individual users and groups will have access to:

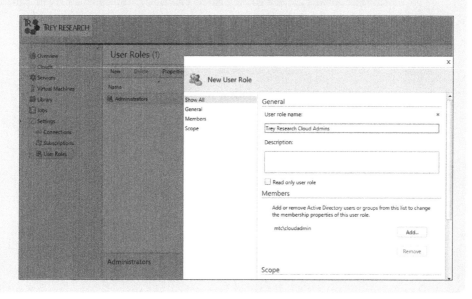

Managing clouds

Once the administrator connects to all the clouds that the organization has access to, the business unit IT administrators and self-service users see the clouds that they have access to, based on the roles defined in Virtual Machine Manager (for private clouds) and App Controller (for hosting service-provider clouds and Windows Azure). The page displays the quota assigned for each cloud, and the current resource utilization, so that you are in a better position to decide where you want to create your next virtual machine or service:

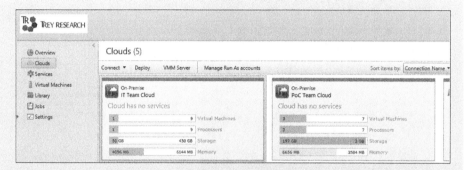

When you are ready to deploy your service or virtual machine, select the cloud where you want the service or virtual machine deployed, and choose from the available templates. The templates shown here are again based on the permissions given in Virtual Machine Manager:

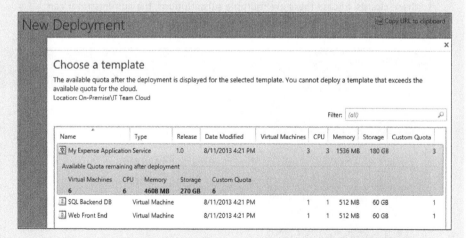

The Services workspace displays all the services deployed to private, public, and service-provider hosted clouds, and it lets you perform administration tasks like start, stop, resume, suspend, shutdown of the service, which in turn will do the corresponding task for all the virtual machines that are part of the template. This is useful for administrators, especially when there are a lot of services deployed.

You can also get a diagram view of a service that gives a visual representation of all the virtual machines that are part of a service and the networks and other virtual machines that they are connected to. When the administrator publishes an update for a deployed service template, a notification appears in the portal and you can update the template at your convenience.

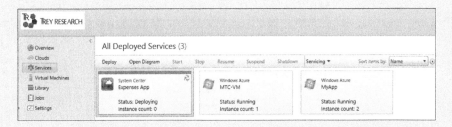

The Virtual Machines workspace displays all the virtual machines that are deployed either as a standalone deployment or as part of a service template. All the virtual machines running on the service-provider hosted cloud as well as the public cloud are also listed in the same page, giving you an overall picture of all the resources that you own or are responsible for from a single page, as well as their current status and resources utilization. Administration tasks like start, shutdown, pause, save, store, mount image, and remote desktop can be performed by selecting the appropriate option:

Performing operations across clouds

One of the biggest benefits of App Controller is the flexibility that it provides administrators to perform operations across clouds using a single management interface. This may be important for different scenarios, like moving a workload temporarily to Windows Azure when you anticipate an increased load, or even to automate the migration using System Center 2012 R2 Orchestrator. With App Controller, this can be achieved by just copying the virtual machine that needs to be moved. The virtual machine that needs to be moved from the private cloud to Windows Azure has to be first shut down and stored in the library. Once the virtual machine is in a stored state, you can copy the virtual machine's disk to Windows Azure, and then create a VM in Azure using that disk.

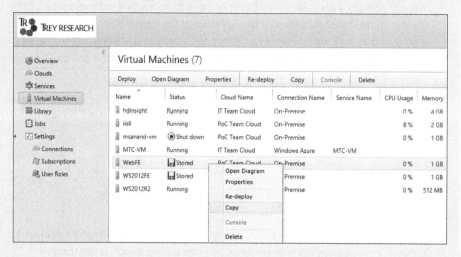

Similarly, you can move a virtual hard disk from Windows Azure to the local virtual machine library by selecting the virtual hard disk from Windows Azure and copying it from there:

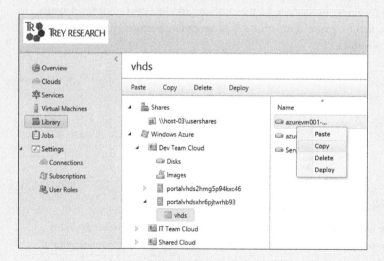

You can then use the Virtual Machine Manager console to deploy the virtual hard disk that has been copied.

MS Anand
Technical Evangelist, Microsoft Technology Center India

How to learn more

The following sections provide links where you can learn more about App Controller.

Product home page

Your starting point for exploring, trying, buying, deploying, and supporting App Controller and other System Center 2012 R2 products is the System Center 2012 R2 home page on Microsoft's Server And Cloud Platform site at *http://www.microsoft.com/en-us/server-cloud/ products/system-center-2012-r2/.*

TechNet Library

If you're already familiar with previous versions of App Controller, you might want to start with "What's New in System Center 2012 R2 App Controller" found at *http://technet.microsoft .com/en-us/library/dn249765.aspx.* If you're new to App Controller, you can browse the full online documentation for App Controller starting from *http://technet.microsoft.com/en-us/ library/hh546834.aspx.*

TechNet wiki

The System Center 2012 App Controller Survival Guide can be found at *http://social.technet .microsoft.com/wiki/contents/articles/7565.system-center-2012-app-controller-survival-guide .aspx.*

TechNet forums

To get answers to your questions about App Controller, try posting to the App Controller - General forum on TechNet at *http://social.technet.microsoft.com/ Forums/en-us/home?forum=appcontroller.*

TechNet Evaluation Center

You can download evaluation versions of App Controller and other System Center 2012 R2 products from the TechNet Evaluation Center at *http://technet.microsoft.com/en-US/evalcenter/ dn205295.*

TechNet Virtual Labs

You can try out App Controller and other System Center 2012 R2 products online using the TechNet Virtual Labs at *http://technet.microsoft.com/en-us/virtuallabs.*

Channel 9

Channel 9 on MSDN has lots of helpful videos on App Controller. See *http://channel9.msdn .com/search?term=App+Controller&type=All*.

Microsoft Virtual Academy

The Microsoft Virtual Academy has online courses on App Controller and other System Center 2012 R2 products at *http://www.microsoftvirtualacademy.com/product-training/system-center*.

CHAPTER 4

Managing and maintaining with Configuration Manager

This chapter provides a brief overview of System Center 2012 R2 Configuration Manager. The topics covered in this chapter include

- Introduction to Configuration Manager
- Configuration Manager in action
- Insights from the experts
- How to learn more

Introduction to Configuration Manager

Configuration Manager provides you with a comprehensive solution for change, configuration, software, and device management. By using Configuration Manager, you can deploy operating systems and applications, deploy software updates, perform hardware and software inventory, ensure compliance through monitoring and remediation, perform remote administration of managed devices, ensure endpoint protection, and manage clients over the Internet.

Configuration Manager overview

Configuration Manager can be used to manage environments of any size, from a handful of computers in one location to hundreds of thousands of different devices distributed around the world. Configuration Manager achieves this flexibility by using a hierarchical architecture based on the concept of sites. A *site* consists of a site server that hosts site system roles and contains resources for managing clients, which can include servers, workstations, laptops, tablets, and mobile devices such as smartphones.

You can use Configuration Manager to create three types of sites: central administration, primary, and secondary sites. For most organizations, even enterprise environments that have thousands of client devices to manage, a single standalone primary site will likely suffice for managing your clients. If your organization has small branch offices connected by a slow network connection to your central office, you might want to deploy secondary sites to manage your clients with a two-level hierarchy of a single primary site and multiple secondary sites. Very large enterprise environments can also deploy Configuration Manager in a three-tier hierarchy that has one central administration site, multiple primary sites, and many secondary sites. The central administration site is not used for managing devices directly; instead, it coordinates intersite data replication across the hierarchy using database replication. The central administration site also facilitates administration of hierarchy-wide configurations for client agents, discovery, reporting, and other operations. The central administration site type was first introduced in Configuration Manager 2012.

Each site has a *site server* that provides the core functionality for the site. Other site system roles can be deployed on the site server or on other servers in the site to support additional Configuration Manager operations. For example, the site database server hosts the Microsoft SQL Server database that stores information about Configuration Manager assets and site data. A management point receives configuration data from clients and provides policy and service location information to clients. A distribution point stores source files such as application content, software packages, software updates, operating system images, and boot images that can be downloaded by managed clients. A reporting services point integrates with SQL Server Reporting Services to create and manage reports. There are more than a dozen different site-system roles in total that each provide a specific type of functionality for managing clients. A number of these roles, including the management point and distribution point roles, can have multiple instances of them installed to help spread the load and support a larger number of clients and for remote forest scenarios.

Installing the Configuration Manager client software on a device enables it to be managed by Configuration Manager. Examples of management operations you can perform on client systems include reporting hardware and software inventory information, deploying operating systems and applications, and pushing out configuration settings for compliance and desired configuration. Configuration Manager client software can be deployed using a variety of methods, including client push installation, software update-based installation, Group Policy, or manual installation. Devices that share a common set of criteria can be logically grouped together into *collections* to simplify management of them. For example, if you want to roll out a new application to all the mobile devices in your environment, you can use the All Mobile Devices collection, and several collections come preinstalled. User collections can also be used to allow delegated users to perform tasks such as installing software or configuring power-management options on their devices. And for devices on which the Configuration Manager client software cannot be installed—for example, certain kinds of mobile devices—limited management of these devices by Configuration Manager is supported through the Microsoft Exchange ActiveSync protocol, which is implemented using the Exchange Server connector.

Configuration Manager solutions

The most widely deployed usage for Configuration Manager today is for managing the end-user device environment of large enterprises, which can consist of desktop PCs, laptops, and other mobile devices such as tablets and smartphones. Many of these organizations have used Configuration Manager as their enterprise client solution since the days when earlier versions of Configuration Manager were still called *Systems Management Server*. Examples of management tasks for PCs and laptops might include operating system deployment, patch management, software inventory, malware protection, compliance, and other functions. Management functionality for other tablets and smartphones is more limited in Configuration Manager and depends on the device type and operating system.

A growing use for Configuration Manager in today's cloud-based business world is for managing servers in the datacenter. This is, in part, because all System Center 2012 R2 components are included in this version, which means that datacenter administrators now have access to powerful client-management tools. Examples of datacenter management tasks include managing infrastructure servers, virtualization hosts, and virtual machines and performing other tasks such as server operating system and enterprise application deployment, server update management, asset management and inventory, and desired configuration and compliance.

We'll explore these two different types of Configuration Manager solutions separately next. Note, however, that from the point of view of Configuration Manager itself, management of end-user devices and datacenter servers is the same—both are simply clients that can be managed using the same infrastructure of sites, site servers, and roles.

Configuration Manager for end-user device management

End-user device management can be a challenge for organizations for several reasons. Businesses often need to manage a wide range of end-user devices. These devices might reside in the workplace, such as desktop PCs, or be handheld mobile devices, such as smartphones. Desktop PCs might be assigned to a single user or shared among many users; mobile devices cannot be shared and must enrolled to a specific user for management by Configuration Manager. If they are a PC, they might be running any version of Microsoft Windows or a third-party operating system like Mac OSX. A tablet might be running Windows, Windows RT, Apple iOS, or Android. A smartphone might be running Windows Phone, Apple iOS, or Android. Note that Configuration Manager does not support managing end-user computers running Linux.

Whatever type of device or operating system is being used and wherever it is found, Configuration Manager provides the necessary change and configuration management functionality you can use to manage your end-user devices. The sections that follow examine six areas of client management functionality provided by Configuration Manager, with the focus here being on managing end-user devices:

- Deployment
- Software updates
- Inventory
- Compliance

- Remote Control
- Endpoint Protection

An additional section examines how Microsoft's Windows Intune cloud-based service can be integrated with Configuration Manager to simplify the management of end-user devices over the Internet.

Deployment

Configuration Manager provides you with tools and infrastructure you can use to create operating-system images and deploy them to Windows-based computers in your environment. Operating system images are Windows Imaging (WIM) format files that contain a version of the Windows operating system together with applications, device drivers, and customizations needed for your environment. When operating-system images are deployed to managed computers to upgrade the operating system on the computers, user-state information is captured and later restored on the targeted computers. Configuration Manager can also be used to create bootable media for deploying operating-system images to unmanaged computers. Integrating the Microsoft Deployment Toolkit (MDT) with Configuration Manager provides additional capabilities for customizing the deployment process, such as creating a customized task sequence for computer deployment, capturing images of Windows 8.1 computers, and using advanced automation capabilities.

Configuration Manager also provides you with tools and infrastructure you can use to create, deploy, manage, and maintain applications in your environment. You can use Configuration Manager to deploy applications to a wide range of end-user devices, including desktop PCs, laptops, tablets, and smartphones. The types of applications you can deploy range from native Windows Installer to Microsoft Application Virtualization (App-V) to third-party app packages for iOS and Android. You can also give users of Windows-based computers control over how and when applications are installed on their devices by publishing them in the Application Catalog, which displays applications available for installation in the Software Center on their computers. For mobile computers, user-targeted software appears in the Company Portal.

Software updates

Configuration Manager provides you with tools and infrastructure you can use to deploy, manage, and monitor software updates on end-user computers in your environment. An effective software-update process helps ensure the security of the computer in your environment. Software updates are retrieved from Microsoft Update and replicated throughout the Configuration Manager hierarchy. Note that deploying software updates is possible only for Configuration Manager clients or Windows clients running Windows Intune, not for mobile devices.

Inventory

Configuration Manager can be used to gather information about the end-user hardware and software throughout your organization. Information gathered from managed clients can be encrypted before sending it to management points to ensure the security and privacy of your environment. You can query the Configuration Manager database to drill down and find detailed information about hardware and software in your organizations. Reports can be generated that can help you make informed decisions when planning upgrades or other IT projects in your environment. You can also use gathered information to make collections to facilitate the management of similar clients. The inventory feature of Configuration Manager is also highly customizable because it is built on Microsoft SQL Server Reporting Services.

Compliance

Configuration Manager provides you with tools and resources you can use to assess, track, and remediate the configuration compliance of end-user devices in your organization. You can use this functionality to ensure that client computers have the correct version of Windows installed and configured correctly, that the correct applications are installed and configured correctly, that system settings such as power management and Windows Update options are configured correctly, and so on. Compliance is evaluated against baselines you define according to the specific needs of your business. You can use the client status feature introduced in Configuration Manager 2012 to monitor the health of clients and check and remediate various problems that might occur. Note that the compliance feature is supported only for Configuration Manager Windows-based clients.

Remote Control

You can use the Remote Control feature of Configuration Manager to view or remotely administer end-user Windows-based computers and to provide assistance to users of client computers in the Configuration Manager hierarchy. This capability can be used by helpdesk personnel to assist users when they have problems they are unable to solve on their own, over the phone, using email, using instant messaging, or using any other communications channel in your organization. The Remote Control feature of Configuration Manager has several advantages over the Remote Desktop and Remote Assistance features of the Windows platform. For example, Remote Control can be used even if there is no user logged on to the target computer. Remote Control also provides the helpdesk with the ability to switch context between different administrators. It also includes the ability for the end user to see what is going on during the session. Usage of Remote Control can also be audited to protect against possible misuse.

Endpoint Protection

You can use System Center 2012 R2 Endpoint Protection to configure antimalware policies and Windows Firewall settings to selected groups of Windows-based computers in your Configuration Manager environment. Endpoint Protection provides detection and remediation for malware, spyware, and rootkits; critical vulnerability assessment and automatic updating of malware definitions and the detection engine; network vulnerability detection; and integration with Microsoft Active Protection Services to report malware to Microsoft.

Beginning with System Center 2012, Endpoint Protection is fully integrated with Configuration Manager and no longer requires a separate installation. The Endpoint Protection dashboard is also integrated with the Configuration Manager console, and Endpoint Protection reports are integrated with the Configuration Manager reporting feature. Note that Endpoint Protection is provided only for Windows clients, not for Mac or Linux clients.

Windows Intune

Windows Intune is a cloud-based service from Microsoft you can use to configure device deployment to manage and secure your organization's information assets over the Internet. The standalone (cloud-only) version of Windows Intune provides you with a web-based administration console you can use to manage Windows, Windows RT, Windows Phone 8, Apple iOS, and Android devices. Windows Intune currently provides only a subset of the management features supported by Configuration Manager. Specifically, you can use Windows Intune to upload and publish software packages, manage policy, track computer inventory, and perform some additional management tasks without the need of implementing an on-premises systems-management infrastructure.

Windows Intune can also be integrated with Configuration Manager to enable you to manage both corporate-owned and personally owned devices using a single management console. Such integration can make it easier for organizations to identify and enforce compliance while enabling a bring-your-own-device (BOYD) approach to allowing personal devices in the workplace. You can use the Windows Intune Connector in Configuration Manager to manage Windows Phone 8, Windows RT, iOS, and Android devices over the Internet.

Configuration Manager for datacenter management

Although Configuration Manager is already widely deployed in enterprises for managing end-user devices, a steadily growing new use for the platform is for managing the virtualized datacenter. Hosting providers can use Configuration Manager in their cloud datacenters for configuring and managing their Hyper-V hosts, for deploying software updates to hosts and virtual machines, and for performing other types of advanced configuration tasks.

Although Configuration Manager is optimized to support client PCs and devices, there are no limitations or restrictions on its ability to run servers and datacenters, and any of the supported platforms can be managed whether they are running on physical hardware or a virtual machine. The sections that follow examine six areas of datacenter management functionality provided by Configuration Manager:

- Deployment
- Software updates
- Inventory
- Compliance and access
- Endpoint Protection
- Linux and UNIX management

Deployment

Configuration Manager provides you with tools and infrastructure you can use to create and deploy operating system images for servers and virtual machines in your environment. It does this using the same technologies as client management, including Windows Imaging (WIM) and the Microsoft Deployment Toolkit (MDT), which offers additional customization capabilities. These server images can also include enterprise applications, OEM device drivers, and additional customizations needed for your environment.

Servers can be organized by group, user, or region to phase a deployment rollout. Servers that are upgraded also have the option to migrate their user state information. Bootable media containing operating system images can also be created, and this can be particularly helpful in datacenters where PXE boot isn't possible. Configuration Manager 2012 R2 can store images as VHD files and optionally place them in a Virtual Machine Manager library share together with App-V packages. Virtual Machine Manager can then use these library objects to deploy preconfigured virtual machines or inject application packages into application profiles and virtual machines.

Software updates

Configuration Manager provides you with tools and infrastructure you can use to deploy, manage, and monitor software updates on servers and virtual machines in your environment. Datacenter administrators can use Configuration Manager to patch and maintain a "master image" of each virtual machine they deploy. This ensures that the virtual machine is secure and stable as soon as it comes online, and additional maintenance cycles are not wasted to bring it up to date.

Inventory

Configuration Manager can be used to gather information about the hardware and software throughout your datacenter to simplify asset management. Administrators often find this helpful when they need to quickly scan their physical infrastructure to locate hardware serial numbers, identify outdated device drivers, or review firmware versions. Detailed information about enterprise application installations can also be helpful to ensure there is consistency across servers. Reports about datacenter components can also be generated to help make informed business decisions.

Compliance and access

Configuration Manager provides you with tools and resources you can use to assess, track, and remediate the configuration compliance of managed servers and virtual machines in your organization. This functions similarly to client compliance management to ensure that settings have not changed, and they can be remediated if they have changed.

Certifying that server settings have not changed is a common task for datacenter administrators—for example, checking whether another administrator might have changed a Server Core installation to a Full installation. If this occurred, the server would no longer be compliant because additional patches would be needed to support the newly added GUI components. Configuration Manager would detect this unauthorized change and could either simply report compliance or perform automatic remediation by running a custom script to uninstall the unauthorized components from the server.

Configuration Manager also enables servers and groups to be managed using role-based administration. This means that different administrators can have access only to specific types of systems, such as client machines, mobile devices, servers, or virtual machines. This can help ensure compliance by preventing unauthorized access to business-critical systems.

Endpoint Protection

Endpoint Protection can be used to configure antimalware policies and Windows Firewall settings to selected groups of servers and virtual machines in your Configuration Manager environment. This can help protect your datacenter servers against threats that might negatively impact your business.

Linux and UNIX management

Configuration Manager also supports managing a variety of Linux server distributions, including Red Hat, SUSE, CentOS, Ubuntu, Debian, and Oracle, along with the AIX, HP-UX, and Solaris UNIX distributions. However, it does not provide all the same management features for these systems as for Windows systems, such as operating-system deployment.

Software distribution to Linux and UNIX systems is supported using packages, but not using the newer application distribution model. Hardware inventory is also similar for these systems, but it gathers the data using an open source equivalent to WMI *called Open Management Infrastructure (OMI)*. (See *http://omi.opengroup.org*.) You can also see what packages are installed on the computer in the native packaging format, such as RPM on Red Hat Linux, but you cannot search the file systems for specific files or file types.

Compliance management for operating-system settings is not possible for these systems; however, client agent settings can be applied for tasks such as scheduling inventory scans and setting maintenance windows to control when software distribution happens.

Endpoint Protection is supported for Linux systems, though it is not integrated into the Configuration Manager console, so a standalone instance must be deployed. However, Linux systems can also be secured using System Center Operations Manager by using the Endpoint Protection Management Pack for Linux, which raises alerts to the Operations Manager console.

All of these various tools and technologies can be used to manage a heterogeneous datacenter, supporting Linux distributions running on Hyper-V, as well as UNIX distributions running on different hypervisors.

Configuration Manager in action

Let's now look at a few examples of Configuration Manager at work. Figure 4-1 shows the Configuration Manager console with the Assets And Compliance workspace selected. This workspace is used to view the compliance of all components managed by Configuration Manager, including Users, Devices, Assets, and more. In this screen shot, the administrator is viewing the overview of the environment, including a compliance error.

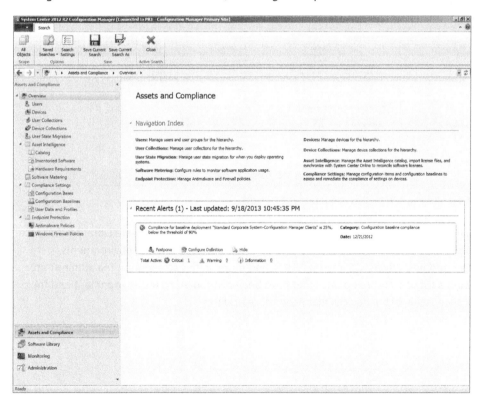

FIGURE 4-1 Reviewing a compliance error in the Configuration Manager console

Figure 4-2 shows the Configuration Manager console with the Assets And Compliance workspace selected. In this screen shot, the administrator is viewing the Devices group and can see the configuration, health, and compliance of a server. Configuration Manager can be used to manage devices running Windows, Linux, UNIX, Mac OS X, Windows Phone, iOS, Android, and Windows Embedded.

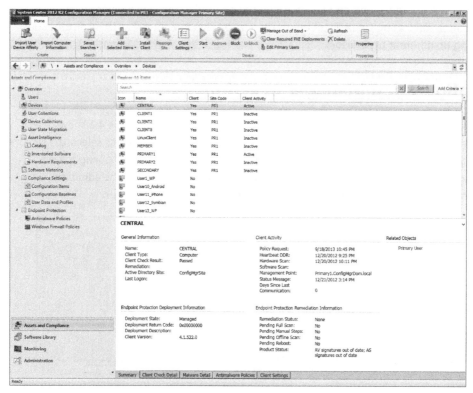

FIGURE 4-2 Viewing information about managed clients

Figure 4-3 shows the Configuration Manager console with the Software Library workspace selected. This workspace is used to manage applications, App-V virtual environments, software updates, drivers, OS images, VHDs, and more. In this screen shot, the administrator is viewing a list of software updates that have been distributed to the environment and the compliance status of the devices that need those updates.

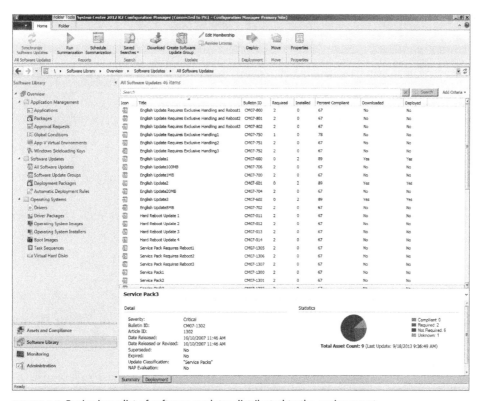

FIGURE 4-3 Reviewing a list of software updates distributed to the environment

Figure 4-4 shows the Configuration Manager console with the Monitoring workspace selected. This workspace is used to report on the health of the environment through raising alerts and generating reports about the sites, systems, deployments, databases, and distribution across the different Configuration Manager servers. In this screen shot, the administrator is configuring the behavior of a compliance alert.

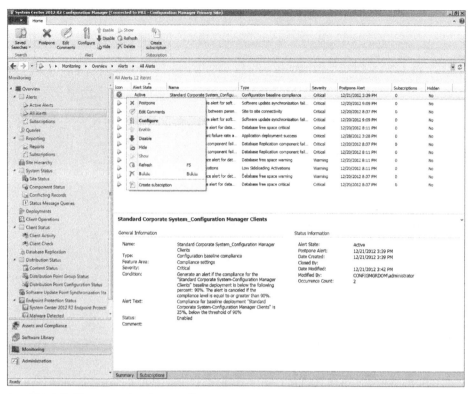

FIGURE 4-4 Setting up an alert for compliance

Insights from the experts

We'll conclude this chapter by hearing from one of our experts at Microsoft about some new features that were added in this release of Configuration Manager.

Content management improvements in System Center 2012 Configuration Manager R2

System Center 2012 Configuration Manager 2012 R2 allows for prioritization of distribution points, which is used by Package Transfer Manager to determine the sending order of content distribution requests. In previous versions of Configuration Manager, when Package Transfer Manager was asked to send content to distribution points, the order was not customizable.

Consider the scenario of an organization with a large number of distribution points across slow wide area network (WAN) links and several distribution points supporting a large user population at a headquarters location. In System Center 2012 Configuration Manager SP1 and earlier, Package Transfer Manager shows no preference regarding WAN speed as it determines the order to send content to distribution points. Because Configuration Manager has a limit on the number of concurrent sendings and threads per package, a handful of slow distribution points can hold up content distribution to the faster distribution points at headquarters.

In comparison, System Center 2012 Configuration Manager R2 gathers information about the speed of previous requests and uses this to prioritize the order in which distribution points receive content. As content is scheduled for sending by Package Transfer Manager, this information is used to ensure content is sent to the fastest distribution points first. The result of this addition is that the fastest distribution points receive content first, followed by slower distribution points.

Also new in System Center 2012 Configuration Manager R2 is the ability to manage "In Progress" content transfers to a downstream distribution point. This functionality is particularly useful when a large package is inadvertently distributed to distribution points and the job needs to be cancelled.

Finally, new in System Center 2012 R2 Configuration Manager, distribution-point usage by clients is now tracked across all distribution points in the enterprise. This data is reported to administrators because it allows for monitoring of distribution-point usage, and it assists in determining if additional or fewer distribution points are required.

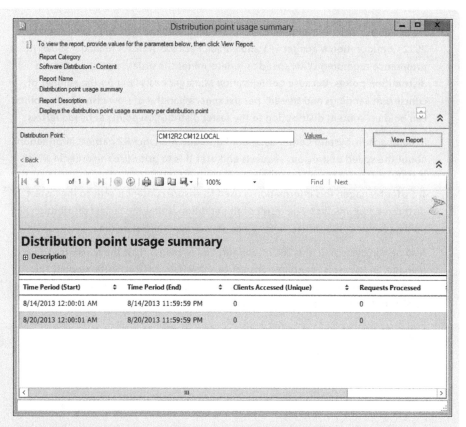

Behind the scenes, this task works similar to validating distribution-point content because it is scheduled to run once a day. A scheduled task executes SMSDPUsage.exe, which will evaluate IIS logs and generate a report of distribution-point usage that is sent to the management point for processing into the database. Similar to the content-monitoring task, the SMSDPUsage executable will create the SMSDPUsage. log file that can be used to verify the task is running and troubleshoot any issues.

Heath Lawson
Premier Field Engineer (http://aka.ms/helawblog)

How to learn more

The following sections provide links where you can learn more about Configuration Manager.

Product home page

Your starting point for exploring, trying, buying, deploying, and supporting Configuration Manager and other System Center 2012 R2 components is the System Center 2012 R2 home page on Microsoft's Server and Cloud Platform site at *http://www.microsoft.com/en-us/server-cloud/products/system-center-2012-r2/*.

TechNet Library

If you're already familiar with previous versions of Configuration Manager, you might want to start with "What's New in System Center 2012 R2 Configuration Manager," found at *http://technet.microsoft.com/en-us/library/dn236351.aspx*. If you're new to Configuration Manager, you can browse the full online documentation for Configuration Manager, starting from *http://technet.microsoft.com/en-us/library/gg682129.aspx*.

TechNet blogs

For the latest information about Configuration Manager, follow the System Center Configuration Manager Team Blog at *http://blogs.technet.com/b/configmgrteam/* and the System Center Configuration Manager Support Team Blog at *http://blogs.technet.com/b/configurationmgr/*. Also, see the Windows Intune Blog at *http://blogs.technet.com/b/windowsintune/* and the Forefront Endpoint Protection Blog at *http://blogs.technet.com/b/clientsecurity/*.

TechNet Wiki

The Configuration Manager wiki articles can be found at *http://social.technet.microsoft.com/wiki/contents/articles/703.wiki-management-portal.aspx#System_Center_Configuration_Manager*.

TechNet forums

To get answers to your questions about Configuration Manager, try posting to one of the Configuration Manager forums on TechNet at *http://social.technet.microsoft.com/Forums/en-US/home?category=systemcenter2012configurationmanager*. Also, be sure to see the System Center 2012 Configuration Manager Survival Guide at *http://social.technet.microsoft.com/wiki/contents/articles/7075.system-center-2012-configuration-manager-survival-guide.aspx*.

TechNet Evaluation Center

You can download evaluation versions of Configuration Manager and other System Center 2012 R2 components from the TechNet Evaluation Center at *http://technet.microsoft.com/ en-US/evalcenter/dn205295*. To try out Windows Intune for 30 days for free, go to *http://www .microsoft.com/en-us/server-cloud/products/windows-intune/default.aspx#fbid=UStC_eU6ZP7*.

TechNet Virtual Labs

You can try out Configuration Manager and other System Center 2012 R2 components online using the TechNet Virtual Labs at *http://technet.microsoft.com/en-us/virtuallabs*.

Channel 9

Channel 9 on MSDN has lots of helpful videos on Configuration Manager. See *http://channel9 .msdn.com/search?term=SCCMandtype=All*.

Microsoft Virtual Academy

The Microsoft Virtual Academy has numerous online courses on Configuration Manager and other System Center 2012 R2 components at *http://www.microsoftvirtualacademy.com/ product-training/system-center*.

Twitter

@ConfigMgrIX is the official Twitter feed of the Configuration Manager documentation team. See *https://twitter.com/configmgrix*.

CHAPTER 5

Backup and recovery with Data Protection Manager

This chapter provides a brief overview of System Center 2012 R2 Data Protection Manager. The topics covered in this chapter include

- Introduction to Data Protection Manager
- Data Protection Manager in action
- Insights from the experts
- How to learn more

Introduction to Data Protection Manager

Data Protection Manager enables you to provide continuous data protection and recovery for your servers. Data Protection Manager can be used to protect files stored in folders and shares or volumes on your file servers. Data Protection Manager can also be used to protect application data on servers running Microsoft Exchange, Microsoft SharePoint, or Microsoft SQL Server, including the SQL databases used by the System Center components. You can use Data Protection Manager to protect both physical and virtual servers in your environment. You can also use it to perform bare-metal recovery (BMR) of mission-critical servers to manage their system state. Data Protection Manager can even be used to protect Windows client computers and computers in workgroups and untrusted domains.

Data Protection Manager works by creating disk-based replicas (copies) of the file and application data on protected servers. These replicas are stored in storage pools that can be implemented using disk storage, tape storage, a mixture of disk and tape, or a secondary Data Protection Manager server, or they can be backed up to the cloud using Windows Azure backup. Storage is synchronized at customizable intervals to ensure that you can quickly recover data when needed.

To protect a computer in your environment, you install the Data Protection Manager protection agent on the computer, and then you add the computer to a protection group, which is a collection of data sources that share the same protection configuration, such as disk allocations, a replica creation method, and a protection policy.

Data Protection Manager uses a SQL Server database to store information about the servers under protection. You can monitor alerts and jobs using the DPM Administrator Console and generate reports showing status, disk or tape utilization, recovery times, and other useful information. As with other System Center components, Data Protection Manager includes its own Windows PowerShell module you can use to automate any data-protection management tasks you can perform from the console.

Protecting virtual machines

One of the key uses for Data Protection Manager is to provide continuous data protection for virtual machines hosted on servers that run Microsoft Hyper-V. Being able to back up virtual machines is essential for any private cloud solution.

One way of protecting virtual machines is to perform a full backup of the Hyper-V host on which the virtual machines run. This approach is recommended because it protects all the data needed to fully restore the host, such as the virtual networks configured on the host, the configuration and virtual hard disk files of the virtual machines on the host, and any snapshots associated with the virtual machines. Another approach to protecting virtual machines is to combine the approaches just mentioned with backups performed from within the guest operating system of each virtual machine.

Data Protection Manager supports both of these scenarios. Installing the protection agent on the Hyper-V host allows you to back up file and application data of the host, including the configuration, virtual hard disks, and snapshots of the virtual machines on the host. Installing the agent on the guest operating system of a virtual machine allows you to back up file and application data on the guest. You can use Data Protection Manager to protect virtual machines hosted on standalone Hyper-V hosts that use local or direct-attached storage (DAS) or Server Message Block (SMB) 3.0 file server storage and on host clusters that use Cluster Shared Volumes (CSV) storage. You can even use it to protect virtual machines that are running during a live migration. Note that online backup of virtual machines is supported for most guest operating systems except for certain older Windows versions. In addition, protection for Linux-based virtual machines is supported but limited to creating file-consistent snapshots.

Installing the Hyper-V server role on the Data Protection Manager server itself provides the additional capability of being able to perform item-level recovery (ILR), which allows you to recover individual files, folders, volumes, and virtual hard disks from a host-level backup. An advantage of using ILR is that the protection agent does not need to be installed on the guest operating system of the virtual machines on the host. Files recovered using ILR can be restored either to a network share or to a volume on a protected server.

Protecting the private cloud

Although Data Protection Manager provides the core functionality you need to be able to back up and restore file and application data in a private cloud environment, you can build a more robust cloud-protection solution by integrating Data Protection Manager with other System Center components. For example, you can integrate the health-monitoring capabilities of Operations Manager with the DPM Administrator Console by using the DPM Management Pack that is included with Data Protection Manager; you can use the System Center Integration Pack for System Center 2012 Data Protection Manager to create workflows in Orchestrator that interact with Data Protection Manager; you can protect the databases of other System Center components using Data Protection Manager; and you can back up Data Protection Manager data to Windows Azure Backup, which provides scalability and elasticity that can simplify and help reduce the cost of managing your backup storage.

Data Protection Manager in action

Let's now look at a few examples of Data Protection Manager at work. Figure 5-1 shows the DPM Administrator Console with the Monitoring workspace selected. This workspace is used to see the status of all Alerts and Jobs from the DPM Server. In this screen shot, the administrator is reviewing the details of a warning that recommends deploying the protection agent to one of the nodes in a cluster.

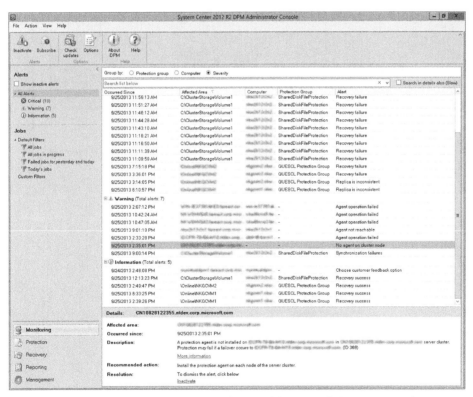

FIGURE 5-1 Viewing alerts in the Monitoring workspace of the DPM Administrator Console

Figure 5-2 shows the DPM Administrator Console with the Protection workspace selected. This workspace is used for configuring the servers, virtual machines, and applications that will be protected. In this screen shot, the administrator is configuring backup for several disks.

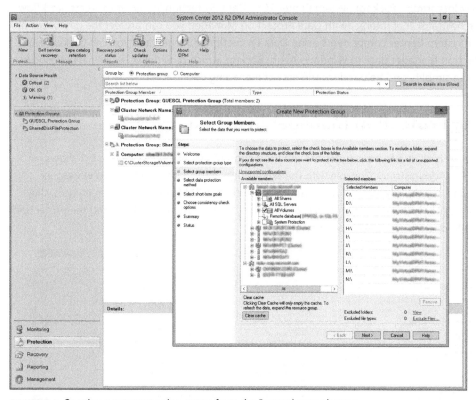

FIGURE 5-2 Creating a new protection group from the Protection workspace

Figure 5-3 shows the DPM Administrator Console with the Recovery workspace selected. This workspace is used for restoring data from backup to several locations. In this screen shot, the administrator is recovering data from a virtual machine and restoring it to a host.

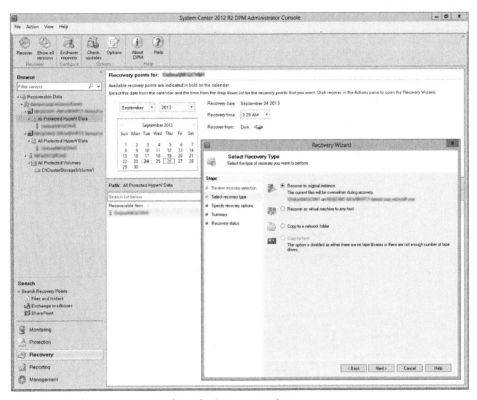

FIGURE 5-3 Performing a recovery from the Recovery workspace

Figure 5-4 shows the DPM Administrator Console with the Reporting workspace selected. This workspace is used for creating reports about the state of the DPM environment. In this screen shot, the administrator is reviewing the Status Report, which provides information about recovery points.

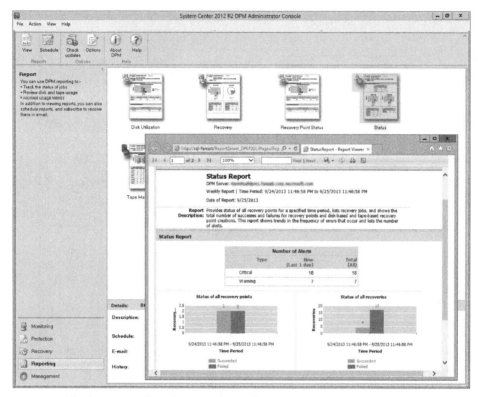

FIGURE 5-4 Viewing a report from the Reporting workspace

Figure 5-5 shows the DPM Administrator Console with the Management workspace selected. This workspace is used for configuring Agents, Disks, Online backup to Azure, and Libraries. In this screen shot, the administrator is installing new protection agents to servers that it will start protecting.

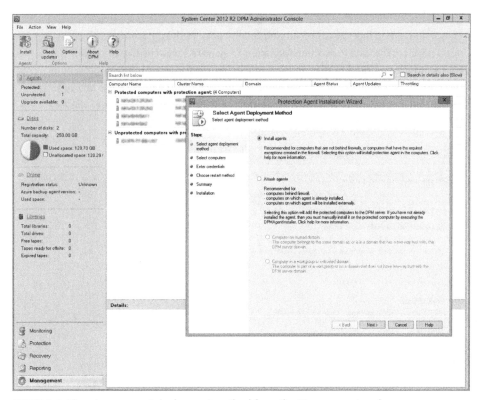

FIGURE 5-5 Choosing an agent deployment method from the Management workspace

Insights from the experts

We'll conclude this chapter by hearing a real-world story from one of our experts at Microsoft about why one of his customers decided to deploy Data Protection Manager.

Solving a backup problem with Data Protection Manager

System Center Data Protection Manager is great for the use case of backing up remote and field office locations. One of my customers had roughly 100 field offices, with a server or two in each location performing file and print functions—each with a tape drive attached. The company's IT department could not afford dedicated IT staff to drive to each site and rotate tapes, so local office administrative staff were trained how to perform the job. This caused a lot of variability and cost with ensuring these sites were protected, so we suggested centralizing backups with Data Protection Manager to a datacenter location.

The customer had link speeds of varying quality back to the datacenters, which is not a problem for Data Protection Manager. They were very sensitive to network congestion and wanted to ensure these offices were not inoperable during backups. Data Protection Manager was the perfect solution for this scenario, as the ability to throttle on a per-computer basis with a unique schedule on each computer was key to success in this situation.

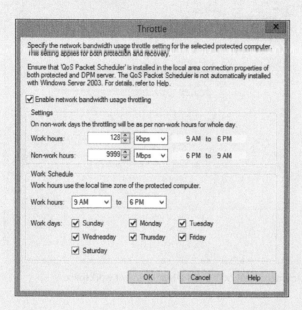

We also wanted to shorten the backup windows—not a problem for Data Protection Manager. Due to how Data Protection Manager follows a continuous protection model, we had the capability to perform frequent synchronizations of data without having to ever take another full backup after the initial backup, as well as the ability to compress the data using excess CPU resources on the field servers with the on-the-wire compression feature included in Data Protection Manager.

Data Protection Manager is very easy to implement and scales well horizontally. The ability to have this backup solution up and running in a very short amount of time with easy expansion capabilities has really made this product appealing to my customers.

Mike Gaal
Datacenter Technology Solutions Professional

How to learn more

The following sections provide links where you can learn more about Data Protection Manager.

Product home page

Your starting point for exploring, trying, buying, deploying, and supporting Data Protection Manager and other System Center 2012 R2 components is the System Center 2012 R2 home page on Microsoft's Server and Cloud Platform site at *http://www.microsoft.com/en-us/server-cloud/products/system-center-2012-r2/*.

TechNet Library

If you're already familiar with previous versions of Data Protection Manager, you might want to start with "What's new in System Center 2012 R2 - DPM" found at *http://technet.microsoft.com/en-us/library/dn296613.aspx*. If you're new to Data Protection Manager, you can browse the full online documentation for Data Protection Manager starting from *http://technet.microsoft.com/en-us/library/hh758173.aspx*.

TechNet blogs

For the latest information about Data Protection Manager, follow the System Center Data Protection Manager at *http://blogs.technet.com/b/dpm/*.

TechNet wiki

The System Center 2012 Data Protection Manager Survival Guide can be found on the TechNet wiki at *http://social.technet.microsoft.com/wiki/contents/articles/11867.system-center-2012-data-protection-manager-survival-guide.aspx*.

TechNet forums

To get answers to your questions about Data Protection Manager, try posting to one of the Data Protection Manager forums on TechNet at *http://social.technet.microsoft.com/Forums/en-us/home?category=dpm*.

TechNet Evaluation Center

You can download evaluation versions of Data Protection Manager and other System Center 2012 R2 components from the TechNet Evaluation Center at *http://technet.microsoft.com/en-US/evalcenter/dn205295*.

TechNet Virtual Labs

You can try out Data Protection Manager and other System Center 2012 R2 components online using the TechNet Virtual Labs at *http://technet.microsoft.com/en-us/virtuallabs*.

Channel 9

Channel 9 on MSDN has lots of helpful videos on Data Protection Manager. See *http://channel9.msdn.com/search?term=VMM*.

Microsoft Virtual Academy

The Microsoft Virtual Academy has numerous online courses on Data Protection Manager and other System Center 2012 R2 components at *http://www.microsoftvirtualacademy.com/product-training/system-center*.

Twitter

@SystemCenter is your official Twitter source for System Center solutions and news. You can find reviews, discussions, and helpful information at *https://twitter.com/system_center*.

Implementing monitoring

Private clouds don't just need to be provisioned; they also need to be monitored to ensure that the services and applications meet the organization's service-level agreement. Two kinds of monitoring are crucial to ensure the availability and performance of cloud solutions. First, you need real-time monitoring so that you can watch the health of your environment and be alerted when something goes wrong. Second, you need proactive monitoring to catch problems before they can cause interruption or poor performance for your business applications.

System Center provides you with both of these capabilities. System Center Operations Manager enables you to monitor in real time the operating systems, services, applications, devices, and operations of the systems and devices in your environment. System Center Advisor allows you to proactively monitor server workloads in your environment to identify potential misconfiguration issues that might cause you problems in the future.

This section of the book provides you with an introduction to Operations Manager Advisor, examines these System Center components in action, provides expert insights from Microsoft insiders, and lists additional resources where you can learn more.

CHAPTER 6

Real-time monitoring with Operations Manager

This chapter provides a brief overview of System Center 2012 R2 Operations Manager. The topics covered in this chapter include

- Introduction to Operations Manager
- Operations Manager in action
- Insights from the experts
- How to learn more

Introduction to Operations Manager

Operations Manager enables you to monitor hardware, virtual machines, operating systems, services, applications, devices, and operations for the systems in a computing environment. Operations Manager can be used to monitor environments for businesses both large and small, in datacenter environments, and for private, public, or hosted cloud solutions. Operations Manager can monitor both client and server systems, displaying health, availability, and performance information collected from these systems within a single console that you can use to detect and resolve real-time problems in your environment. Monitored systems can be running a version of Microsoft Windows, a supported version of the Linux or UNIX operating systems, and a variety of third-party infrastructure servers, such as the VMware and Citrix virtualization platforms.

The basic unit of management functionality for Operations Manager is the *management group*, which consists of one or more management servers, a reporting server, and two databases. The operational database contains the configuration data for the management group. The data warehouse database contains the historical monitoring and alert information collected from the systems being monitored. The reporting server generates reports from the information stored in the data warehouse database. The management server administers the management-group configuration and databases, and it collects information from the systems being monitored.

Operations Manager uses agents to collect information from the systems you want to monitor in your environment. After you deploy and configure Operations Manager, the next step is to decide which systems should be monitored and which services, applications, and other features should be monitored on these systems. Agents must then be deployed on targeted systems so that the systems can be monitored using the console. The agent is a service running on the system that collects information, compares the information to predefined values, and generates alerts and runs responses. Agent software can be deployed using push installation (discovery) or from installation media; the discovery method requires that certain firewall ports first be opened on the targeted systems. Operations Manager also supports agentless monitoring by allowing the collection of performance and availability information from a system that does not have an agent installed by using a proxy agent that is installed on another system.

Management packs

A key feature of Operations Manager is the *management pack*. Management packs extend the monitoring capabilities of Operations Manager by enabling it to monitor a specific application or service. They include discovery information that enable a management server to automatically detect and start monitoring target systems, an internal knowledge base that contains error and troubleshooting information for diagnostic and troubleshooting purposes, rules for generating alerts and events, tasks that can be performed by either the agent or console, reporting capabilities, and other features. Management packs can be easily created and customized, enabling you to monitor almost any datacenter hardware or software component, including your own company's line-of-business applications and services.

When Operations Manager is installed, a number of management packs are also installed. These management packs provide core monitoring functionality, including operating-system monitoring for Windows, Linux, and UNIX; application monitoring; network monitoring; a collection of auditing information; reporting; notifications; and other monitoring capabilities. Additional management packs are available from the catalog on the Microsoft System Center Marketplace and can be imported into Operations Manager from the console to extend the management capabilities of the platform. You can find the Microsoft System Center Marketplace at *http://systemcenter.pinpoint.microsoft.com/en-US/home*.

Monitoring tools and scenarios

Operations Manager can be used to monitor operating systems, services, and applications running on systems. Operations Manager provides two types of consoles for monitoring your environment: a Microsoft Management Console (MMC)-based console and a web console. You can use the MMC-based console to perform any actions that your assigned user role allows. The web console displays only My Workspace and the Monitoring workspace. The Monitoring workspace displays a summary of the health of distributed applications and systems in your environment by showing state and alert information for each monitored component. Other tools provide additional functionality—for example, Health Explorer helps you diagnose problems in your environment by viewing alerts and state changes and taking action on them.

Operations Manager can be used to monitor web applications built using the Microsoft .NET Framework or Java. Web applications can be monitored from both the server-side and client-side perspectives to collect information about performance and reliability by analyzing the application at the code level. The information gathered can then be used to help you and your developers identify the root causes of application failure or poor application performance in your environment.

Operations Manager also can be used to discover and monitor routers, switches, firewalls, and load balancers on your physical network, and it can use that information to generate network topology diagrams showing how the systems are interconnected. This provides you with visibility into the health and performance of your network infrastructure that can help you identify when application or service failures are caused by network problems.

Operations Manager also can be used to monitor Windows servers that have been configured as failover clusters. The Microsoft Windows Cluster Management Pack provides discovery and monitoring of cluster shared volumes.

Monitoring the private cloud

Operations Manager plays a key role in private cloud solutions built using the System Center platform by helping to ensure the reliable offering of cloud services. You can use Operations Manager to measure the resource demands of cloud services so that you can properly size and distribute resources for optimal performance. You can also use it to measure the health of your cloud fabric and of services deployed in your cloud. Detailed reports can be generated that summarize the performance and availability of your cloud services.

Operations Manager also integrates closely with several other components of the System Center platform and can be integrated with third-party monitoring solutions from IBM, HP, BMC, and others. Operations Manager 2012 R2 maintains the same connector framework as Operations Manager 2007 R2. These connectors can be used to synchronize alerts between Operations Manager and other monitoring tools. For example, Service Manager includes a connector that allows Operations Manager objects to be automatically imported as configuration items in Service Manager and another connector that allows alerts generated by PRO-Enabled management packs to be imported into Service Manager. And a connector for System Center Advisor is available that lets you view Advisor alerts in the Operations Manager console.

Beginning with System Center 2012, however, the preferred method for synchronizing alert data between Operations Manager and other monitoring-systems connectors is to use Orchestrator runbooks. The advantage of using runbooks for this purpose is that Orchestrator provides greater third-party extensibility that can support a wider range of monitoring systems. See the section "Integration packs" in Chapter 9 for more information on this functionality.

Virtual Machine Manager integrates directly with Operations Manager so that you can display Operations Manager information and manage management packs from within the Virtual Machine Manager console. PRO-Enabled management packs (*PRO* stands for *Performance and Resource Optimization*) enable Virtual Machine Manager to perform automated actions in response to particular conditions determined from information collected by Operations Manager. The Microsoft System Center Virtual Machine Manager management pack lets you monitor the availability of Virtual Machine Manager along with the availability, health, and performance of all virtual machines and virtual machine hosts being managed by Virtual Machine Manager. Integrating Operations Manager 2012 R2 with Virtual Machine Manager 2012 R2 also provides you with a Fabric Health Dashboard in Operations Manager that provides a detailed overview of the health of your private cloud and also the fabric that services those clouds. By integrating Operations Manager with Virtual Machine Manager, you can quickly see the health of your cloud and its underlying fabric and virtual machines

Operations Manager in action

Let's now look at a few examples of Operations Manager at work. Figure 6-1 shows the Operations Manager console with the Monitoring workspace selected. This workspace is used to provide details of the health of any component managed by Operations Manager, including hardware, servers, business applications, virtual machines, or customer applications. In this screen shot, the administrator is reviewing the details of a warning about the memory on a Hyper-V host.

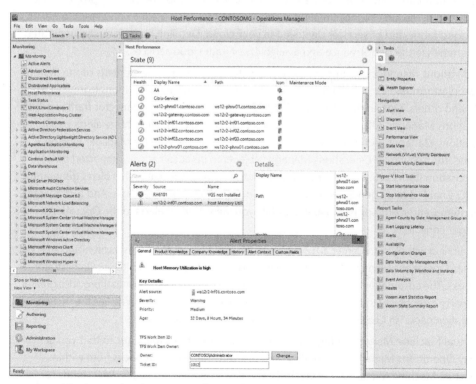

FIGURE 6-1 Viewing an alert for a Hyper-V host in the Operations Manager console

Figure 6-2 shows the Operations Manager console with the Authoring workspace selected. This workspace is used to create and configure management packs, management pack objects, distributed applications, and groups. In this screen shot, the administrator is configuring a global service monitor for a web application, which allows the website to be tested for availability and performance from different Microsoft points of presence located around the world.

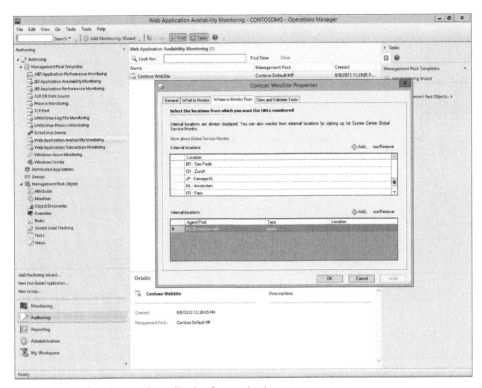

FIGURE 6-2 Configuring a web application for monitoring

Figure 6-3 shows the Operations Manager console with a diagram view of the health of a distributed System Center service. The diagram views can give a quick visual tip to help identify managed systems with issues. In this screen shot, the administrator is reviewing the health of the System Center Data Access Service and is able to quickly identify the errors with the databases and web user interfaces.

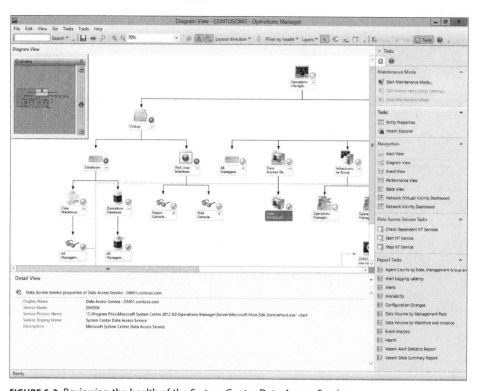

FIGURE 6-3 Reviewing the health of the System Center Data Access Service

Figure 6-4 shows the Operations Manager console with the Administration workspace selected. This workspace is used to configure a variety of monitoring settings, including devices, management packs, network management, notifications, UNIX/Linux accounts, security, and more. In this screen shot, the administrator has launched the Computer And Device Management Wizard to add some new network devices under management.

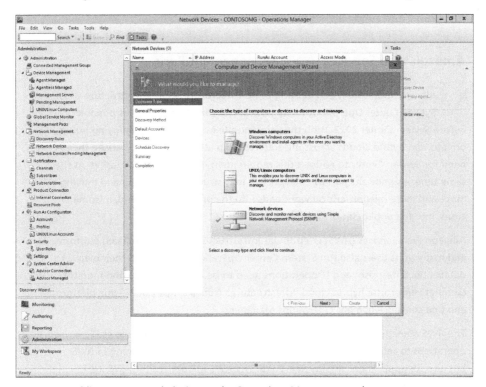

FIGURE 6-4 Adding new network devices to the Operations Manager console

Insights from the experts

We'll conclude this chapter by hearing from some of our experts at Microsoft. First, here are two experts talking about a capability supported by Operations Manager—namely, the monitoring of public and hybrid cloud infrastructure with the new Amazon Web Services (AWS) Management Pack for Operations Manager 2012 R2.

Amazon Web Services (AWS) Management Pack

Multilayer monitoring and alerting of non-Microsoft cloud infrastructure with System Center Operations Manager was not something that was possible before System Center 2012. With the rising number of customers deploying public, private, and hybrid clouds across different cloud platforms, there has arisen the need for System Center to address this requirement in this changing market. At the same time, a significant part of enterprise IT infrastructure is evolving and moving more and more mission-critical workloads into the private cloud—and, in some cases, into the public cloud.

Amazon Web Services (AWS) is a popular Infrastructure as a Service (IaaS) platform, and many of its users also run System Center Operations Manager in their own datacenter. Enterprises and IT operations need to be able to manage and monitor complete enterprise hybrid cloud infrastructures from a single point—one platform and one console—namely, Operations Manager.

The AWS Management Pack (MP) for Operations Manager 2012 R2 allows IT operations to set up multilayer monitoring not only for services running in AWS but also for applications deployed in AWS. The AWS MP utilizes the AWS .NET SDK to remotely access the AWS CloudWatch management service in order to collect information about allocated virtual infrastructure, resources, and real-time performance metrics.

Cloud platform monitoring

The most important part of the AWS MP capabilities is discovering and monitoring resources centered on availability and performance information for the following AWS services:

- EC2 (Elastic Compute)
- Elastic Block Storage (EBS)
- Elastic Load Balancers (ELB)
- CloudFormation Stacks (CF)
- Autoscaling

CloudWatch metrics are surfaced as performance counters, and associated alarms are surfaced in Operations Manager as alerts and also fed into the health models for the EC2, EBS, ELB, Autoscaling, and CloudFormation stacks. The AWS MP discovers and links Amazon EC2 instances and the Windows and Linux operating systems running on those EC2 instances. Only EC2 instances running the System Center Operations Manager agent will participate in this linking.

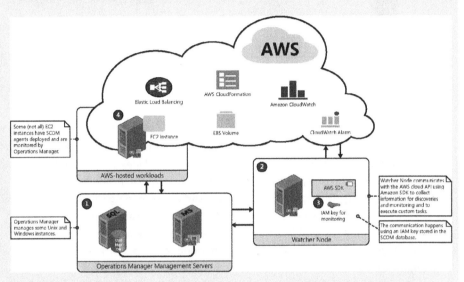

The preceding diagram illustrates how cloud platform monitoring is implemented with Operations Manager and the AWS MP. We define the model of "levels" where the AWS MP, standard MPs, and other third-party MPs operate. The first Level "0" (the Infrastructure of AWS EC2 and other AWS service components) is where AWS MP primarily manages. The second level ("Level 1," the operating systems, and applications level) is also managed by the AWS MP and common SCOM MPs today. Level 1 entities "link" with Level 0 entities (Infrastructure). The Level "2" entities are represented by the other AWS services and are surfaced as health models in Operations Manager 2012 R2. However, only by enabling both the AWS MP and standard SCOM MPs does the customer really gain the advantage of the full, end-to-end picture of the health of their infrastructure in the cloud.

Enterprise services monitoring

At the same time, IT operations used to get an advantage from end-to-end monitoring models that implemented major Operations Manager MPs such as SQL MP, Exchange MP, or SharePoint MP, where administrators could build one health model over another. Additionally, it afforded them the ability to pay attention only to the top levels of a health hierarchy, with the ability to drill down to a failed element through health rollups. The AWS MP implements the same approach.

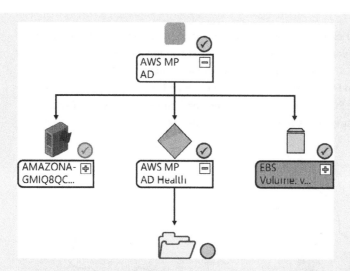

As the preceding diagram illustrates, when an Operations Manager administrator deploys Operations Manager agents to AWS virtual machines, she automatically turns on the health rollup between the guest operating system and guest services (for example, SQL DB deployed in the cloud) and corresponding elements of the AWS infrastructure monitored by the AWS MP. In this case, the monitoring capabilities of AWS CloudWatch and the power of management packs for services work together and provide a powerful monitoring scenario, which is not available anywhere else.

Chris Samson
Senior Partner Technology Strategist, Microsoft

Roman Yuferev
Business Manager, VIAcode Consulting LLC

Now let's hear from another of our experts at Microsoft—this time concerning the Microsoft Monitoring Agent, a new agent in Operations Manager 2012 R2 that replaces the Operations Manager Agent in previous versions of the platform.

Microsoft Monitoring Agent

The Operations Manager Agent is a well-known service for those who are using Operations Manager on a daily basis. This service has been renamed several times before. When Operations Manager 2007 was first released, this service was called OpsMgr Health Service. By the time of 2007 R2, it had changed to System Center Management, and from 2012 R2 to the present we've been calling it Microsoft Monitoring Agent (or MMA).

The main purpose of Microsoft Monitoring Agent is to monitor and collect operative information about managed computers and applications and send that data back to management servers for further processing. In addition to the well-known Operations Manager monitoring engine (Health Service), it also contains the .NET Application Performance Monitoring (APM) module, which was introduced in System Center 2012 and can be used to collect IntelliTrace logs from web applications that are running on Internet Information Services (IIS) 7.0, 7.5, or 8.0.

For those who are familiar with previous versions of Operations Manager, I've summarized most of the notable changes in the following table:

Property	2007 R2	2012 and 2012 SP1	2012 R2
OM Agent service name	System Center Management	System Center Management	Microsoft Monitoring Agent
Default install path	%ProgramFiles%\System Center Operations Manager	%ProgramFiles%\System Center Operations Manager\Agent	%ProgramFiles%\Microsoft Monitoring Agent\Agent
Control Panel object name	N/A	Operations Manager Agent	Microsoft Monitoring Agent
Version	6.0.7221.0	7.0.9538	7.1.10133.0
APM	N/A	Included	Included
APM service name	N/A	System Center Management APM	Microsoft Monitoring Agent APM
ACS Forwarder service name	Operations Manager Audit Forwarding Service	System Center Audit Forwarding	Microsoft Monitoring Agent Audit Forwarding
IntelliTrace Collector	N/A	N/A	Included

Deploying Microsoft Monitoring Agent

If you ever designed or deployed Operations Manager environments, there is no surprise about the system requirements. We support running Microsoft Monitoring Agent on a lot of operating systems, from Windows XP to Windows Server 2012 R2 on x86 and x64 CPU architecture, but there is no support running on Windows Vista and Windows 7. Almost all Microsoft products have a built-in PowerShell module, and the .NET Framework is going to be a more common component for applications. Microsoft Monitoring Agent is no exception. Detailed system requirements can be found on the Download Center page at *http://www.microsoft.com/en-us/download/details.aspx?id=40316*.

Microsoft Monitoring Agent can be installed in the standard ways, including using console-based push install, manual install, GPO-based install, System Center Configuration Manager, or another software-distribution technology. You can upgrade existing agents using console-based updates or manual updates. Before System Center 2012 R2, the Operations Manager Agent service usually had to be connected to at least one management group for it to run; however, Microsoft Monitoring Agent can work without being attached to an existing management group, which is done to support the IntelliTrace Collector functionality. The installation wizard shows the following options during manual installation:

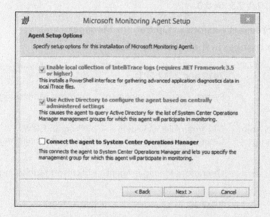

Note that the first check box is grayed out so that the IntelliTrace Collector is installed by default. The only thing that can be configured during manual setup is the Operations Manager Management Group properties.

Using IntelliTrace

First, what is IntelliTrace? IntelliTrace is a feature of Microsoft Visual Studio that allows you to collect runtime trace information that can be replayed through Visual Studio to step through the code. What is incredible is its ability to collect a trace of live, production applications where traditional debugging or tracing is not an option or is not allowed to be used. For more information, visit *http://msdn.microsoft.com/en-us/magazine/ee336126.aspx*.

There are several ways to utilize IntelliTrace. One is to use the command-line tool IntelliTraceSC.exe, which is located in the %ProgramFiles%\Microsoft Monitoring

Agent\Agent\IntelliTraceCollector folder. *SC* here stands for *Standalone Collector*. This tool can be used to collect a trace of .NET 2 or higher managed applications. Keep in mind that Silverlight applications, Windows Phone applications, .NET 1 applications, and Native code applications cannot be traced with IntelliTrace.

The other way to utilize IntelliTrace is to use the Windows PowerShell cmdlets that can be used for tracing IIS-based web applications. To do this, import the IntelliTrace PowerShell module with the following command:

```
Import-Module 'C:\Program Files\Microsoft Monitoring Agent\Agent\
IntelliTraceCollector\Microsoft.VisualStudio.IntelliTrace.PowerShell.dll'
```

After import, the relevant commands are available and you can type **Get-Help intellitrace** to learn what you can do. The following cmdlets are available:

```
Checkpoint-IntelliTraceCollection
Get-IntelliTraceFileInfo
Start-IntelliTraceCollection
Get-IntelliTraceCollectionStatus
Stop-IntelliTraceCollection
```

You can use Get-Help to learn more about these cmdlets.

Marton Csiki
Microsoft Consulting Services, Hungary

How to learn more

The following sections provide links where you can learn more about Operations Manager.

Product home page

Your starting point for exploring, trying, buying, deploying, and supporting Operations Manager and other System Center 2012 R2 components is the System Center 2012 R2 home page on Microsoft's Server And Cloud Platform site at *http://www.microsoft.com/en-us/server-cloud/products/system-center-2012-r2/*.

TechNet Library

If you're already familiar with previous versions of Operations Manager, you might want to start with "What's New in System Center 2012 R2 Operations Manager" found at *http://technet.microsoft.com/en-us/library/dn249700.aspx*. If you're new to Operations Manager, you can browse the full online documentation for Operations Manager starting from *http://technet.microsoft.com/en-us/library/hh205987.aspx*.

TechNet blogs

For the latest information about Operations Manager, follow the Operations Manager Engineering Blog at *http://blogs.technet.com/b/momteam/*.

TechNet wiki

The System Center 2012 Operations Manager Survival Guide can be found in the TechNet wiki at *http://social.technet.microsoft.com/wiki/contents/articles/7809.system-center-2012-operations-manager-survival-guide.aspx*. Other wiki articles on Operations Manager can be found at *http://social.technet.microsoft.com/wiki/contents/articles/703.wiki-management-portal.aspx#System_Center_Operations_Manager*.

TechNet forums

To get answers to your questions about Operations Manager, try posting to one of the Virtual Machine Manager forums on TechNet at *http://social.technet.microsoft.com/Forums/systemcenter/en-us/home?category=systemcenteroperationsmanager*.

TechNet Evaluation Center

You can download evaluation versions of Operations Manager and other System Center 2012 R2 components from the TechNet Evaluation Center at *http://technet.microsoft.com/en-US/evalcenter/dn205295*.

TechNet Virtual Labs

You can try out Operations Manager and other System Center 2012 R2 components online using the TechNet Virtual Labs at *http://technet.microsoft.com/en-us/virtuallabs*.

Channel 9

Channel 9 on MSDN has lots of helpful videos on Operations Manager. See *http://channel9.msdn.com/search?term=SCOM&type=All*.

Microsoft Virtual Academy

The Microsoft Virtual Academy has numerous online courses on Operations Manager and other System Center 2012 R2 components at *http://www.microsoftvirtualacademy.com/product-training/system-center*.

Twitter

@SystemCenter is your official Twitter source for System Center solutions and news. You can find reviews, discussions, and helpful information at *https://twitter.com/system_center*.

CHAPTER 7

Proactive monitoring with Advisor

This chapter provides a brief overview of System Center 2012 R2 Advisor. The topics covered in this chapter include

- Introduction to Advisor
- Advisor in action
- Insights from the experts
- How to learn more

Introduction to Advisor

While Systems Center Operations Manager enables you to monitor your private cloud or datacenter infrastructure in real time, System Center Advisor takes a more proactive approach to monitoring. Unlike other System Center components, which can be installed locally on servers in your on-premises environment, Advisor is a free cloud service from Microsoft that you can access via a web browser at *http://www.SystemCenterAdvisor.com*. Advisor can be used to analyze installations of Microsoft server workloads in your local environment in order to identify potential misconfiguration issues that might cause you problems in the future.

Advisor works by collecting information from agent software running your on-premises Windows servers, securely uploading this information to the Advisor web service via a gateway server deployed in your environment, analyzing the information by comparing it to a set of rules known as *Advisor knowledge*, and raising alerts for you when an issue is found or a deviation from best practices has been identified. Alerts and associated remediation guidance can then be viewed by using a web browser to connect to the Advisor web portal running in the cloud. Examples of Advisor alerts might be things like missing software updates on servers, poor configuration choices that might lead to performance problems, lack of backups being performed, critical services not running or features not enabled, database consistency errors, and so on.

Currently, Advisor can be used to proactively monitor servers running Windows Server 2008 and 2008 R2, Microsoft Hyper-V Server 2008 R2, Windows Server 2012 and 2012 R2, or Microsoft Hyper-V Server 2012 and 2012 R2 as their operating system. Certain versions of server workloads like Microsoft SQL Server, Microsoft Exchange Server, Microsoft Lync Server, and Microsoft SharePoint also can be analyzed, as well as System Center 2012 SP1 Virtual Machine Manager. The Advisor knowledge is built from real customer support cases and regularly updated to support new patches, best practices, platforms, and workloads.

Integration with Operations Manager

Although Advisor can be implemented as a standalone monitoring solution as described in the preceding section, it also can be used together with Microsoft System Center. A key value proposition for customers using System Center 2012 SP1 Operations Manager (with Update Rollup 2+) in their environment is that Advisor can be integrated with Operations Manager. Such integration combines the real-time monitoring capabilities of Operations Manager with the proactive monitoring functionality of Advisor to create a single, comprehensive monitoring solution for the customer's environment.

Integration of Advisor with Operations Manager allows alerts and associated remediation guidance generated by Advisor to be displayed in the Operations Manager console (both the MMC-based and web consoles). While a standalone Advisor solution requires deployment of an on-premises gateway server, the integrated approach does not and instead uses Advisor as an attached service in Operations Manager. With the integrated approach, Advisor uses the existing Operations Manager agent software running on your servers and sends the information it collects to the management servers in your Operations Manager infrastructure. The management servers then use the Advisor connector to upload the information collected to the Advisor web service running in the cloud. The uploaded information is then analyzed by the web service, and any alerts generated are raised in the Operations Manager console so that you can take remedial action concerning them.

Advisor in action

Let's now look at a few examples of Advisor at work. Figure 7-1 shows the Advisor configuration page within Operations Manager with the Advisor Connection settings selected. This is used to configure the connection between Operations Manager and Advisor, running as a cloud-based service. In the screen shot, the administrator is reviewing some alerts that have been previously ignored so that they do not appear again.

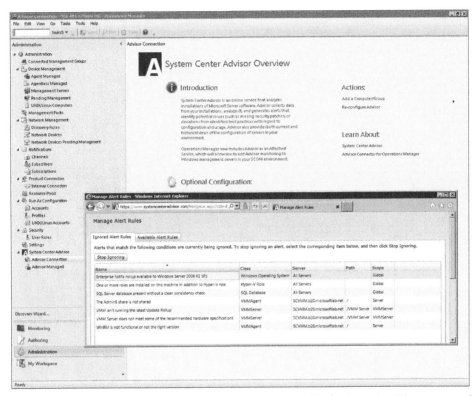

FIGURE 7-1 Reviewing Advisor alerts that were previously ignored in the Operations Manager console

Figure 7-2 shows the health of Advisor's agents within the Operations Manager Monitoring workspace. This workspace is used to view the health of the management server and the various other servers Advisor is analyzing. In this screen shot, the administrator is reviewing the configuration settings of a management server.

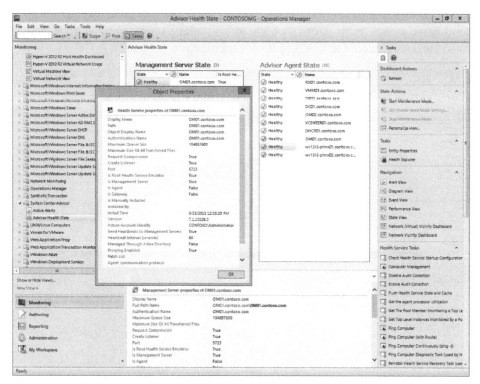

FIGURE 7-2 Reviewing the configuration of a management server

Figure 7-3 shows the Advisor alerts within the Operations Manager Monitoring workspace. This workspace is used to report best practices that are not being followed in the environment. In this screen shot, the administrator is reviewing a critical alert saying that a Virtual Machine Manager server is using an evaluation version that will expire shortly.

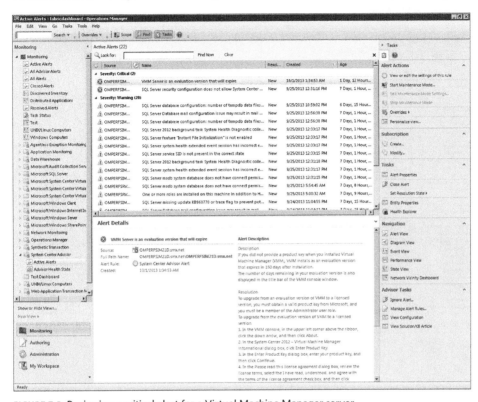

FIGURE 7-3 Reviewing a critical alert for a Virtual Machine Manager server

Figure 7-4 shows the details of the Advisor alerts within the Operations Manager Monitoring workspace. In this screen shot, the administrator is reviewing the details of a warning that recommends changing a SQL Server permission. The administrator then assigns this alert to the engineering team using Team Foundation Server so that the change request will be tracked and made.

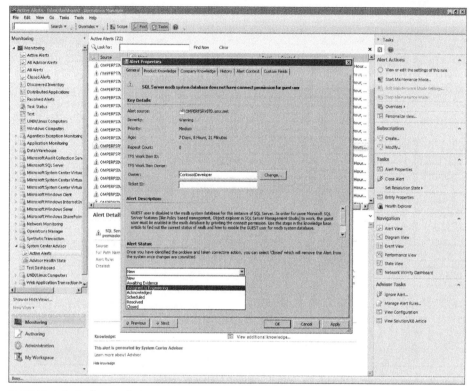

FIGURE 7-4 Assigning an alert to a team

Figure 7-5 shows the details of an active alert within the Operations Manager Monitoring workspace. In this screen shot, the administrator is reviewing a warning that recommends applying an update to avoid several SQL query errors. After clicking the View Solution/KB Article link, the administrator is taken directly to the webpage to download the update and remediate the problem.

FIGURE 7-5 Viewing more details concerning an alert

Insights from the experts

We'll conclude this chapter by hearing from one of our experts at Microsoft about how to get started with using Advisor.

Microsoft's best-kept secret

System Center Advisor is still one of the best kept secrets out there. This free online service will allow you to assess your server configuration and proactively avoid problems while helping you resolve issues faster by putting current and historical configuration at your fingertips.

As of the time of writing this sidebar, Advisor is available for the following products:

- SQL Server 2008, SQL Server 2008 R2, and SQL Server 2012
- Windows Server 2008, Windows Server 2008 R2, and Windows Server 2012
- Windows Server 2008 R2 Hyper-V
- Microsoft Hyper-V Server 2012
- Exchange Server 2010
- SharePoint Server 2010
- Lync Server 2010 and Lync Server 2013
- System Center 2012 SP1 Virtual Machine Manager

The Advisor service itself is developed and maintained by the Microsoft System Center Product Group in partnership with the Microsoft Customer Service and Support (CSS) Escalation Engineers. The beauty of this partnership is that the rules are developed by the support experts who work with thousands of enterprise customers globally. They strive to create Advisor rules for the top issues that they see customers encounter with Microsoft products. Our goal is to learn from the support calls that we see and author rules to prevent more customers from experiencing these known issues. The Advisor rules are regularly updated to continually push new and relevant guidance.

How the Advisor web service works

The System Center Advisor web service is hosted in Windows Azure and works in conjunction with a lightweight on-premises software installed in your local environment. The on-premises software consists of one gateway and at least one agent. The agent collects data from your server and analyzes it using a set of rules (similar to a management pack in System Center Operations Manager) known collectively as Advisor knowledge. The analyzed data is regularly sent from the agent to the gateway for upload to the Advisor web service. If the data indicates an issue or a deviation from best practices, an alert is generated. By connecting a web browser to the Advisor portal, you can view the alerts and the associated remediation guidance:

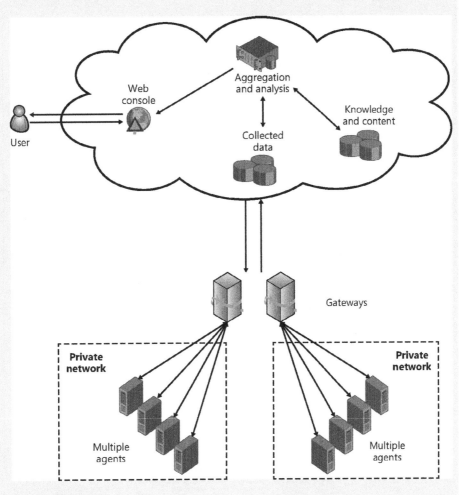

Getting started

You can be up and running in no time with Advisor. How you use it depends on whether you are also running System Center Operations Manager (SCOM) 2012. We'll cover the SCOM attached scenario in a bit.

To create an account, just navigate to *http://www.SystemCenterAdvisor.com*. From there, you can create an account using your Microsoft account or an organizational account:

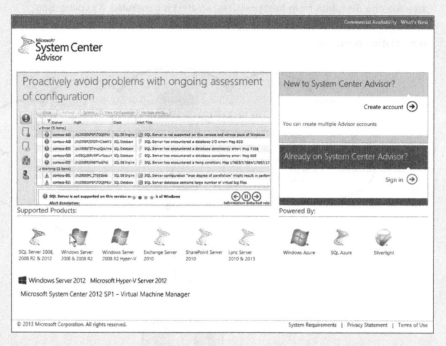

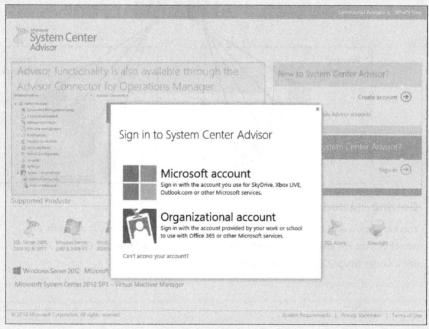

Once you've configured Advisor by installing the gateway and agents, data will begin to be sent to the Advisor service, where it is processed. The resulting recommendations will begin to appear in the Advisor portal. This data will be both environmental information as well as alerts in the form of a warning or an error. Let's walk through what the portal looks like when you log in. The first screen will give you an overview of the environment, showing you warnings and errors by workload as well as the five most recent alerts.

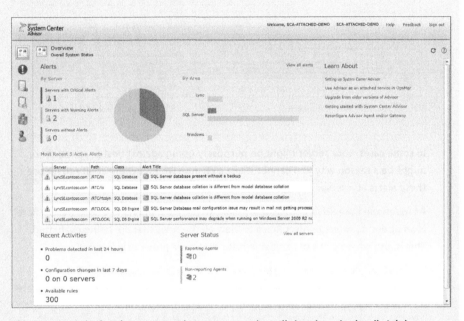

The next page is the alerts page, where you can view all the alerts in detail. Advisor is meant to be an easy-to-use tool to help save you time. The alerts are concise but actionable, and they all have a link to external content specifically written for the issue that was detected. The alert will also highlight the parameters detected as well. For example, as you can see in the following picture, the alert doesn't simply state that a SQL update is required, but it lists the currently installed version. Once the issue is resolved in the environment, the alert will close itself automatically; however, you do have the ability to manually close it if you prefer.

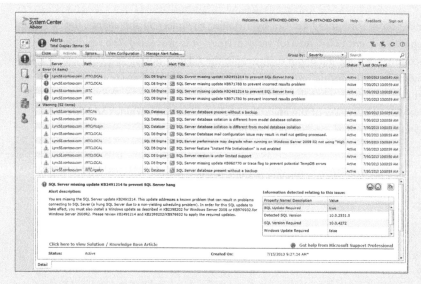

In some cases, your server might be purposely going against best practice; there might be a reason why you cannot make a change. You have the ability to ignore these alerts at a server or organizational level.

As mentioned previously, Advisor is meant to be actionable and transparent. There is an option to Manage Alert Rules to view all the rules that are being evaluated. This is also where you can re-enable rules that were previously ignored.

The next screen will show you the current configuration snapshot for the deployment. You can easily change the context to focus on different servers where an Advisor agent is installed to view the relevant information.

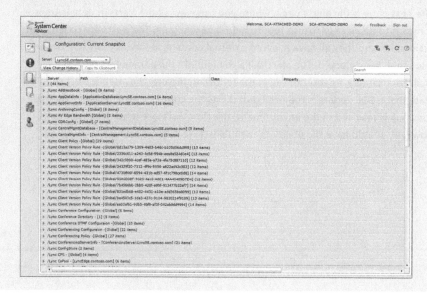

Finally, the feature that is my personal favorite is Change History. Since Advisor performs discovery every 12 hours by default, it has unique knowledge about what has changed in the environment. If you're like most IT pros, the first question you probably ask when troubleshooting an issue is "What changed?" Well now you have a tool to help answer that question. The following example shows a quick search for "QoS" because I was curious to see when the Quality of Service setting was enabled in my Lync Server environment. Advisor quickly shows me the date that the change was first detected!

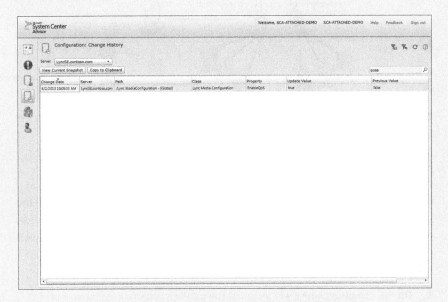

Advisor as an attached service in Operations Manager

Until now, I described how Advisor works with the use of a gateway to communicate to the Advisor service. If you are running Operations Manager 2012 SP1 (plus Update Rollup 2), you can use Advisor as an attached service. Here, the agents will communicate directly with the management server, which will, in turn, communicate with the Advisor service. This allows you to use Operations Manager as your one-stop shop for monitoring. You have your real-time monitoring capability with Operations Manager, and your best-practices recommendations from Advisor. In addition to having all the alerts in a central location, you can now take advantage of the Operations Manager features with Advisor alerts. The picture on the following page details how this all works.

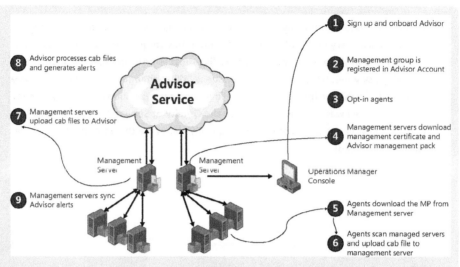

To read more about the prerequisites needed in order to use Advisor as an attached service, refer to *http://technet.microsoft.com/en-us/library/dn168861.aspx*.

Common questions

The most common question we get from customers is around data privacy. One of the great things about Advisor is that you can audit everything that is sent up to the service. Each agent stores the collected information in a set of XML files on the disk. Every 24 hours, these XML files are packaged into a compressed CAB file and copied to the gateway or management server and then uploaded to your Advisor account. You can view these XML files by using the following steps:

1. On the computer where you installed the gateway, open a command-line window.

2. Change to the %programfiles%/SystemCenterAdvisor/GatewayData/ Mailboxes/<agentGUID>/FromAgent directory.

3. Use the expand.exe command to extract the XML files from the .cab file.

4. Open the XML files in an XML editor.

Uploaded files are archived on-premises for five days by default, but you can configure this by changing the following registry value:

Key: HKEY_LOCAL_MACHINE\Software\Microsoft\SystemCenterAdvisor\Gateway

Setting: ArchivePeriod

Type: REG_DWORD

You can read the full privacy statement at *http://onlinehelp.microsoft.com/en-us/ atlanta/gg288262.aspx*.

The other question we typically get is around the performance impact of having agents installed on your servers. While we always recommend testing any software before installing it on production servers, it's important to note that a core design tenant of Advisor is to have low processing overhead. You can expect <1% average CPU with occasional spikes. The agents also have a small memory footprint (<75 MBs) and will upload ~150 kb of data per server per day.

Summary

System Center Advisor is a great service available to you completely free. It's easy to deploy and allows you to identify issues before they cause an outage or impact users. You can benefit from the collective wisdom of the global Microsoft Customer Service and Support teams. I encourage you to visit *http://www.SystemCenterAdvisor.com* to get started!

Nick Rosenfeld
Principal Escalation Engineer (Lync/Skype) at Microsoft

How to learn more

The following sections provide links where you can learn more about Virtual Machine Manager.

Product home page

Your starting point for using System Center Advisor is *https://www.systemcenteradvisor.com/.*

Online Help

Online help for Advisor can be found at *http://onlinehelp.microsoft.com/en-us/advisor/default .aspx.* For the latest news about Advisor, see "What's New in System Center Advisor?" at *http://onlinehelp.microsoft.com/en-us/advisor/gg697799.aspx.*

Channel 9

Channel 9 on MSDN has lots of helpful videos on Advisor. See *http://channel9.msdn.com/ search?term=Advisor&type=All.*

Microsoft Virtual Academy

The Microsoft Virtual Academy has numerous online courses on Advisor and other System Center 2012 R2 components at *http://www.microsoftvirtualacademy.com/product-training/ system-center.*

Twitter

@SystemCenter is your official Twitter source for System Center solutions and news. You can find reviews, discussions, and helpful information at *https://twitter.com/system_center.*

Building private clouds

Once infrastructure has been provisioned, and monitoring is in place, you're ready to build your private cloud. System Center 2012 R2 provides you with tools for doing this. The result will be a transformed datacenter that can bring big benefits to your business.

System Center Service Manager provides you with an integrated platform for delivering IT as a service through automation, self-service, standardization, and compliance. System Center Orchestrator enables you to create and manage workflows for automating cloud and datacenter management tasks. And Windows Azure Pack lets you implement the Windows Azure self-service experience right inside your own datacenter using your own hardware.

CHAPTER 8

Standardization with Service Manager

This chapter provides a brief overview of System Center 2012 R2 Service Manager. The topics covered in this chapter include

- Introduction to Service Manager
- Service Manager in action
- Insights from the experts
- How to learn more

Introduction to Service Manager

IT isn't just about technology, it's also about the people and processes that use those services. Employees don't care about which Microsoft Exchange Server their Microsoft Outlook client gets their mail from, they just need to be able to get their mail so that they can do their job. They also don't want to know the details of how mail servers are upgraded or patched, they just want the newest capabilities without any service interruptions. From the user's perspective, IT just delivers a service they depend on as they perform their daily routine.

The design goal of System Center Service Manager is to provide organizations with an integrated platform for delivering IT as a Service (ITaaS) through automation, self-service, standardization, and compliance. Service Manager does this by enabling

- Automation of IT Service Management (ITSM) processes, such as activity management, change management, incident management, problem management, and release management as defined by industry-standard frameworks like Microsoft Operations Framework (MOF), Information Technology Infrastructure Library (ITIL), and Control Objectives for Information and Related Technology (COBIT). Service Manager provides automation interfaces you can use for automating the delivery of IT services and processes. Service Manager also provides a centralized configuration management database (CMDB), an OLAP-based data warehouse built on Microsoft SQL Server that integrates with other System Center products for centralized data storage.

- Self-service for users by providing a self-service portal (known as the Service Manager Portal or "SMPortal") that allows consumers of IT services to submit requests and view their status, search the knowledge base, and perform other tasks. The self-service portal is customizable and is built on top of Microsoft SharePoint. Service Manager also provides customizable dashboards and reporting based on SQL Server Reporting Services (SSRS) that can provide both real-time and historical information for the service desk.

- A standardized experience for implementing ITSM processes according to standardized frameworks. Service Manager uses templates for defining business processes, and you can build and customize these templates to meet the specific needs of your business through GUI-based wizards, so no coding is required.

- Compliance by logging every service management action in a database so that it can be reviewed and analyzed when needed. Compliance can be continuously evaluated in real time against a predefined baseline, and incidents can be automatically generated when deviation from the baseline is detected.

Service Manager architecture

Service Manager uses a component-based architecture that provides for flexible deployment options. The main components of Service Manager include the following:

- **Service Manager management server**   This server runs the Service Manager engine and is used for managing work items such as incidents, requests, or changes; and for managing tasks and users.

- **Service Manager database**   This is where configuration items, work items, and Service Manager configuration settings are stored. This is the Service Manager implementation of a CMDB.

- **Service Manager Data Warehouse management server**   This server performs management functions for the Service Manager data warehouse.

- **Service Manager Data Warehouse databases**   These are used for long-term storage and reporting of the business data generated by Service Manager.

- **Service Manager console**   This is an administrative console that the service desk can use to manage incidents and change requests, examine metrics, generate reports, and perform other tasks.

- **Self-service portal**   This is a web interface that end users can use to create requests, search for knowledge, and read announcements from the service desk, often called the "SMPortal."

The various Service Manager components can generally be installed on a single server as a lightweight scenario or for testing purposes, or they can be deployed across several servers to support larger and more complex environments; however, the Service Manager database and the Service Manager data warehouse databases must be located on separate servers. Information can be imported from Active Directory Domain Services to prepopulate the Service Manager database. Hardware and software inventory information and software updates can be imported from System Center Configuration Manager. Alerts can be imported from System Center Operations Manager to create incidents in Service Manager. Virtual machine templates and service templates can be imported from System Center Virtual Machine Manager. System Center Orchestrator runbooks can be synchronously invoked from within Service Manager to take advantage of the advanced automation capabilities of Orchestrator. Service Manager can also work with Microsoft Exchange to enable mail to be used for managing the life cycle of Service Manager work items. Service Manager uses various built-in connectors for importing information from (and in some cases, exporting information to) these different data sources. Third-party ITSM solutions can also coexist and communicate with Service Manager through Orchestrator integration.

Extending the platform

Service Manager uses management packs to extend its capabilities, and to export and import data between Service Manager implementations. Management packs allow Service Manager to preserve and separate customer-specific configurations and customizations from the underlying Service Manager engine. A management pack contains information such as classes, workflows, views, forms, reports, and knowledge used to implement specific service-management processes. Management packs are XML-based and can contain both configurations (such as implementing incident categorization) and customizations (such as adding an On Behalf Of field to a change request form).

Service Manager includes a number of predefined management packs that are sealed (cannot be modified) for enabling core functionality for the product, such as incident-management and change-management capabilities. Service Manager includes several unsealed (customizable) management packs for enabling certain optional features of the product, such as some preconfigured views and reports. You can also create your own management packs using the Service Manager Authoring Tool, Visual Studio, Blend for Visual Studio, or other XML editors and development tools. There are also a large number of community-developed management packs available.

Building automation

A workflow is a sequence of activities, actions, or tasks in Service Manager, such as the copying of documents from one system to another as a part of an automated business process. In earlier versions of Service Manager, the primary tool for building workflows was the Service Manager Authoring Tool. Beginning with Service Manager 2012, however, Microsoft recommends that Orchestrator be implemented with Service Manager. Orchestrator is a workflow-management solution you can use to automate the creation, monitoring, and deployment of resources in your environment. Orchestrator 2012 and later includes an Integration Pack for common Service Manager activities, such as editing an incident and creating an object. This approach to Service Manager workflow automation requires less management overhead, provides better error handling, and requires less knowledge of Windows PowerShell scripting.

Service Manager solutions

Microsoft has seen customers deploy Service Manager for two broad areas of solutions:

- **IT Service Management**   Service Manager is frequently used as an organization's help desk solution for supporting IT services provided to employees. IT departments frequently use Service Manager for incident management and request fulfillment. Service Manager can also be used for non-IT service management—for example, for handling room requests made to facility management or for requesting a new credit card from the accounting department. With its capacity for standardized service delivery and its ability to manage multiple processes and provide insights and analysis for service-level agreements (SLA) and operational-level agreements (OLA), Service Manager can fulfill a broad range of service management needs for organizations of all sizes.

- **Self-service for the cloud tenant**   Service Manager has also been deployed in multitenant environments, so its self-service portal can be used to empower end users and free up the time of the IT department by standardizing and automating repetitive tasks. For example, a tenant could use the self-service portal to report an incident such as a virtual networking issue, request a resource such as additional cloud storage, provision a new virtual machine from a template, and so on. Workflows can be created by the hoster to automate the approval process for requests to align with the businesses processes implemented by the hoster. While System Center App Controller provides a self-service experience for deploying and managing virtual machines and services in cloud environments, Service Manager provides additional self-service capabilities that can handle almost any type of service request.

Service Manager in action

Let's now look at a few examples of Service Manager in action. Figure 8-1 shows the Service Manager Console with the Administration workspace selected. This workspace is used to configure a variety of Service Manager settings, including announcements, chargeback, cloud services, connectors to other System Center components, management packs, notifications, security, service-level objectives, workflows, and more. In the following screen shot, the administrator is setting the default configuration of new incidents.

Figure 8-2 shows the Service Manager Console with the Library workspace selected. This workspace contains collections of resources that can be reused in deployments, including knowledge articles, lists, queues, runbooks, request offerings, and service offerings. In the screen shot, the administrator is reviewing a request offering that is published in the Service Manager Console.

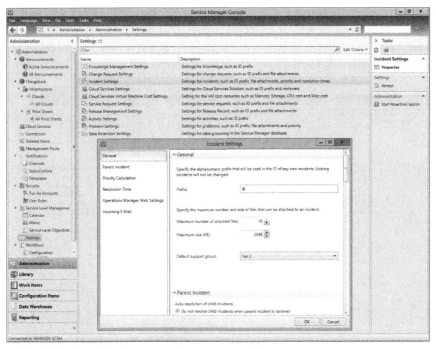

FIGURE 8-1 Configuring the settings for an incident

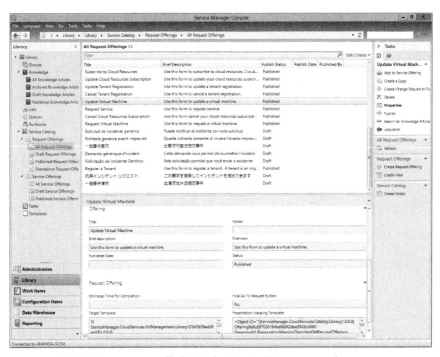

FIGURE 8-2 Reviewing a request offering in the Service Manager console

Figure 8-3 shows the Service Manager Console with the Work Items workspace selected. This workspace serves as a helpdesk for managing activities, changes, incidents, problems, releases, and service requests. In the screen shot, the administrator is reviewing a recent incident about a Virtual Machine Manager agent not being monitored.

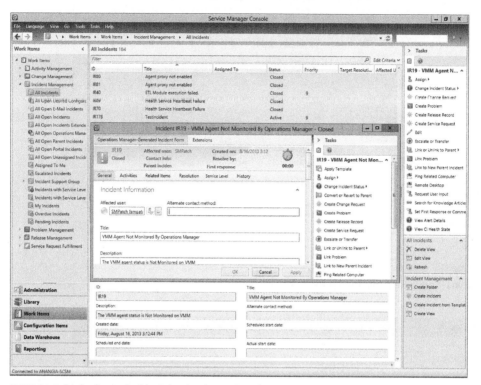

FIGURE 8-3 Reviewing an incident that has been closed

Figure 8-4 shows the Service Manager Console with the Configuration Items workspace selected. This workspace is used to store information about business services, cloud services, computers, printers, software, and software updates that can be used in forms. In the screen shot, the administrator is reviewing a Virtual Machine Manager service template of a Service Manager deployment. The administrator then creates a new related service request, which associates that service template with a Request Virtual Machine request offering.

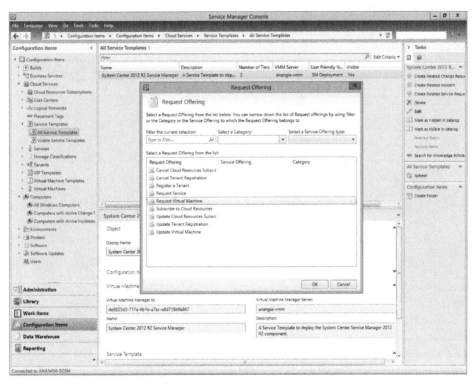

FIGURE 8-4 Creating a new related service request

Figure 8-5 shows the Service Manager Console with the Data Warehouse workspace selected. This workspace is used to manage large quantities of data and transform it into useful reports. In the screen shot, the administrator is reviewing the different dimensions of the chargeback cube before generating a report.

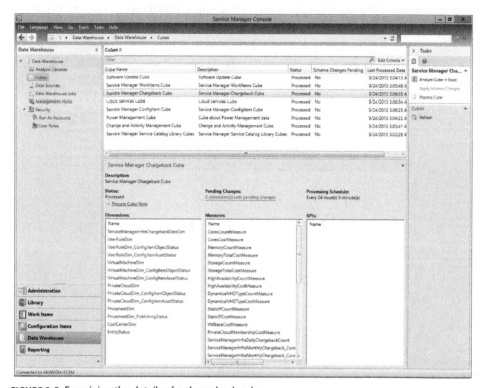

FIGURE 8-5 Examining the details of a chargeback cube

Figure 8-6 shows the Service Manager Portal with the self-service user creating a service request. The Service Manager Portal is a web-based, self-service portal that publishes services and requests that are created in Service Manager. In the screen shot, the administrator is requesting a new virtual machine to be provisioned.

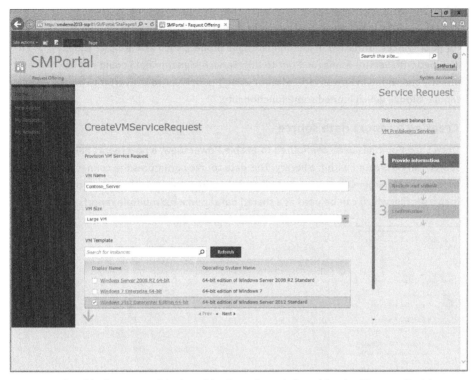

FIGURE 8-6 Provisioning a new virtual machine from the web-based Service Manager Portal

Insights from the experts

We'll conclude this chapter by hearing from one of our experts at Microsoft about how you can get the most from using Service Manager.

Power View for Service Manager dashboards

The release of Cumulative Update 4 (CU4) for SQL Server 2012 Service Pack 1 brought the ability to create Power View dashboards using data from the Service Manager data warehouse. This offers an excellent method of presenting, analyzing, and reporting on Service Manager data in a visually appealing way.

Power View uses SQL Server Reporting Services to create presentation-ready, interactive dashboards that can be published directly to SharePoint. These dashboards can easily be built from within SharePoint using the same skills used to create a Service Manager report in Microsoft Excel. Once designed, the Power View report can be shared with your organization via a SharePoint PowerPivot gallery.

The release of CU4 for SQL Server 2012 SP1 included the ability to use Power View for data sources formatted in multidimensional models, such as the OLAP cubes included with Service Manager. Prior to this, Service Manager data could not be directly consumed in Power View without using PowerPivot to convert it to a tabular model, which limited some functionality.

Creating a report data source

Once SharePoint has been configured to enable Power View, a new report data source can be created within a library. This data source configures the connection to the Service Manager OLAP cube, as well as the credentials used. The output of this is an .rsds file, which can be used as a shared data source for multiple reports.

The report data source needs to be configured as a connection type. For System Center Service Manager, the Microsoft BI Semantic Model For Power View option is used. A connection string is also required, which points to the Service Manager OLAP cube. Because there are many OLAP cubes available in the Service Manager data warehouse, a report data source can be created for each.

The following connection string will connect to DW.Contoso.com, which hosts the SQL Server Analysis Services OLAP cubes for Service Manager and connects to the Work Items cube:

```
Data source=dw.contoso.com;initial catalog=DWASDataBase;
cube='SystemCenterWorkItemsCube'
```

Creating a Power View report

Once the report data source has been saved to a document library, you can click on the ellipsis (...) and select Create Power View Report from the menu.

This will open the Silverlight-based Power View design experience. This is where the dashboard can be created directly in Internet Explorer. The dimensions and measures from the OLAP cube are shown in the Field List. These can be selected to begin building the report in the same way as demonstrated in an Excel PivotTable.

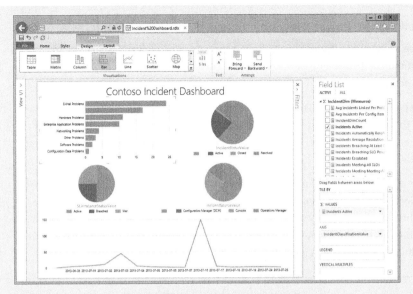

As an example, to show all active incidents by classification category, you simply expand IncidentDim (Measures) and select Incidents Active, and then you expand IncidentDim_Incident Classification and select IncidentClassificationValue. Doing this will generate a table displaying active incidents by classification. The visualization tools in Power View can now be used from the ribbon. By selecting Design, you can change this table to display other formats, such as a bar or pie chart. Each Power View report can contain multiple views, added by simply clicking the New View button. These views are similar to slides in a PowerPoint presentation, merging several dashboards into a single presentation.

Saving to a PowerPivot gallery

After you finish designing the dashboard, it can be saved to SharePoint using the disk icon in the top left corner. If this is saved to a SharePoint PowerPivot Gallery, it will provide the ability to have an attractive and intuitive page, showcasing all of your presentation-ready Service Manager dashboards.

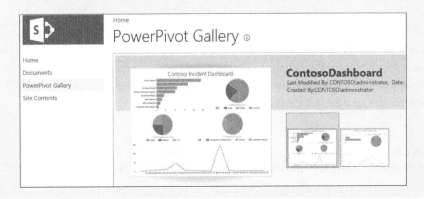

Viewing the Power View dashboard

Once saved to the PowerPivot Gallery, a report can be viewed by clicking on a thumbnail. This will open Power View in reading mode, giving an immersive full-screen experience.

After the report is open, the refresh button in the top left corner can be clicked to get the most recent data from the Service Manager data warehouse. The viewer can easily move between views, alter the presentation size, or change to full-screen mode.

One of the most powerful features of Power View is filtering. Because Power View understands the underlying data model and relationships, filtering one part of a report will automatically update the whole view. For example, clicking on E-Mail Problems from the Incidents Active bar chart will filter the Incident Status pie chart, highlighting only E-Mail incidents.

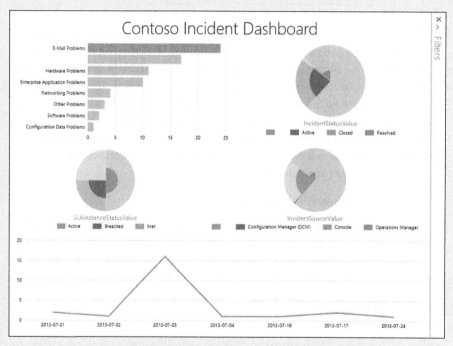

This ability to filter and highlight the report in real time allows you to analyze Service Manager data to understand trends, identify service improvement opportunities, and extract the highest possible value from the data warehouse.

Rob Davies
Premier Field Engineer in the Datacenter Management team at Microsoft

How to learn more

The following sections provide links where you can learn more about Virtual Machine Manager.

Product home page

Your starting point for exploring, trying, buying, deploying, and supporting Service Manager and other System Center 2012 R2 components is the System Center 2012 R2 home page on Microsoft's Server and Cloud Platform site at *http://www.microsoft.com/en-us/server-cloud/products/system-center-2012-r2/*.

TechNet Library

If you're already familiar with previous versions of Service Manager, you might want to start with "What's New in System Center 2012 R2 Service Manager," found at *http://technet .microsoft.com/en-us/library/dn299380.aspx*. If you're new to Service Manager, you can browse the full online documentation for Virtual Machine Manager starting from *http://technet.microsoft.com/en-us/library/hh305220.aspx*.

TechNet blogs

For the latest information about Service Manager, follow the System Center Service Manager Engineering Blog at *http://blogs.technet.com/b/servicemanager/*.

TechNet wiki

The Service Manager wiki articles can be found at *http://social.technet.microsoft.com/wiki/contents/articles/703.wiki-management-portal.aspx#System_Center_Service_Manager*. See especially the Service Manager Survival Guide at *http://social.technet.microsoft.com/wiki/contents/articles/822.service-manager-survival-guide.aspx*.

TechNet forums

To get answers to your questions about Service Manager, try posting to one of the Service Manager forums on TechNet at *http://social.technet.microsoft.com/Forums/systemcenter/en-us/home?category=virtualmachinemanager*.

TechNet Evaluation Center

You can download evaluation versions of Service Manager and other System Center 2012 R2 components from the TechNet Evaluation Center at *http://technet.microsoft.com/en-US/evalcenter/dn205295*.

TechNet Virtual Labs

You can try out System Center 2012 R2 components online using the TechNet Virtual Labs at *http://technet.microsoft.com/en-us/virtuallabs*.

Channel 9

Channel 9 on MSDN has lots of helpful videos on Service Manager. See *http://channel9.msdn .com/search?term=SCSM&type=All*.

Microsoft Virtual Academy

The Microsoft Virtual Academy has numerous online courses on Service Manager and other System Center 2012 R2 components at *http://www.microsoftvirtualacademy.com/ product-training/system-center*.

Twitter

@SystemCenter is your official Twitter source for System Center solutions and news. You can find reviews, discussions, and helpful information at *https://twitter.com/system_center*.

CHAPTER 9

Automation with Orchestrator

This chapter provides a brief overview of System Center 2012 R2 Orchestrator. The topics covered in this chapter include

- Introduction to Orchestrator
- Orchestrator in action
- Insights from the experts
- How to learn more

Introduction to Orchestrator

System Center Orchestrator can be used to create and manage workflows for automating cloud and datacenter management tasks. These tasks might include automating the creation, configuration, management, and monitoring of IT systems; provisioning new hardware, software, user accounts, storage, and other kinds of resources; and automating various IT services or operational processes.

Orchestrator provides end-to-end automation, coordination, and management using a graphical interface to connect diverse IT systems, software, processes, and practices. Orchestrator provides tools for building, testing, and managing custom IT solutions that can streamline cloud and datacenter management. Orchestrator also facilitates cross-platform integration of disparate hardware and software systems in heterogeneous environments.

Orchestrator is a key component of System Center for building private clouds because it allows you to connect complex actions or processes and make them into single tasks that can then be run automatically through scheduling or in response to service requests from customers or users. Orchestrator is also a valuable tool for automating complex, repetitive tasks in traditional datacenter environments and can simplify the management of a large, heterogeneous datacenter.

How Orchestrator works

Orchestrator automates tasks and processes using runbooks. A *runbook* is a logical representation of a sequence of activities that orchestrates a *workflow*, a series of actions that take place against targeted systems, networks, and other resources.

(See Figure 9-2 later in this chapter for an example of a workflow.) Runbooks can be created using the Runbook Designer, a graphical tool that uses drag-and-drop functionality to quickly and easily connect different actions, like running a program, sending an email message, getting the status of a process, monitoring an event log for a specified event, and so on. The different actions are known as *activities* and are organized by the system into what are known as *integration packs*, which are collections of custom activities that are specific to a product or a technology. Integration packs can be created to connect any system that has a programmatic interface, including Microsoft Exchange, Microsoft SharePoint, System Center, Microsoft Windows Azure, VMware, and more.

Once created and tested, runbooks can be checked into the orchestration database, after which the runbook can be triggered to perform its intended task. Each request to run a runbook creates a new *job* in the orchestration database, and a new *instance* of the job is created when a runbook server processes the job.

The components of an Orchestrator deployment are as follows:

- **Runbook Designer**   A graphical design tool that lets you create new runbooks, configure the activities in a runbook, modify the activities in a runbook, and perform other runbook management tasks.

- **Runbook Tester**   A tool that lets you validate and test the runbooks you create.

- **Runbook Server**   One or more servers that run the service that manages runbooks and runs instances of runbooks.

- **Deployment Manager**   A tool used to deploy runbook servers, Runbook Designer instances, and integration packs.

- **Orchestration Database**   The database that stores Orchestrator configuration information, logs, runbooks, and jobs. The orchestration database can be deployed on either Microsoft SQL Server or Oracle.

- **Management Server**   The server that provides communications between the orchestration database and the Runbook Designer.

- **Orchestration Web Service**   A REST-based web service that lets you use applications and scripts to start and stop runbooks and retrieve information about their operations.

- **Orchestration Console**   A web-based tool you can use to view a list of runbooks and runbook servers, view the current status and history of runbooks, start and stop runbooks, and view events related to runbook servers. The functionality of the Orchestration console is a subset of those of the Runbook Designer.

Extending Orchestrator using integration packs

Out of the box, Orchestrator includes over 40 built-in standard activities for building runbooks that automate workflows. A wide range of integration packs are also available for Orchestrator that can extend its workflow-building capabilities with new management functions by integrating Orchestrator with other products and platforms.

Orchestrator integration packs are available for Active Directory, Microsoft Exchange, Microsoft SharePoint, and Windows Azure to enable automation of IT systems and processes that use these Microsoft products and platforms. Integration packs are also available for integrating Orchestrator with other System Center components, including different versions of System Center Configuration Manager, System Center Operations Manager, System Center Virtual Machine Manager, System Center Service Manager, and System Center Data Protection Manager. Integration packs are also available for various third-party platforms and products, including IBM Tivoli, HP Operations Manager, HP Service Manager, VMware vSphere, BMC Remedy, CA ServiceDesk, Cisco UCS, Dell AIM, and more.

See the "How to learn more" section at the end of this chapter for information on where you can find out more about the integration packs currently available for Orchestrator. Developers can also create custom integration packs for in-house applications and systems using the Orchestrator Integration Toolkit, which can be downloaded using the link found in the "How to learn more" section at the end of this chapter.

Orchestrator in action

Let's now look at a few examples of Orchestrator in action. Figure 9-1 shows the Orchestrator Deployment Manager with the Integration Packs workspace selected. Integration packs contain a collection of activities (actions or tasks) that enable Orchestrator to provide integration across diverse systems. This workspace is used to add new integration packs to the servers that design and execute workflows. In this screen shot, the administrator is reviewing the details of the VMware vSphere integration pack.

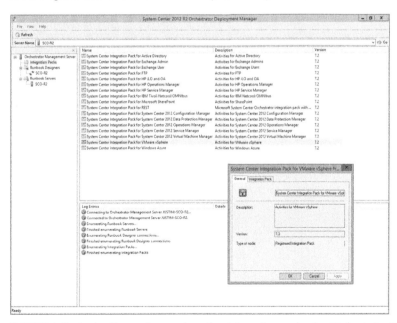

FIGURE 9-1 Reviewing the version number of an integration pack using Orchestrator Deployment Manager.

Figure 9-2 shows the Orchestrator Runbook Designer with the Runbooks workspace selected. This workspace is used to design the actions, parameters, and execution order of the activities from the integration packs. In this screen shot, the administrator is reviewing a runbook that inputs data, executes scripts, collects information about different user roles, and then integrates a VMware vSphere server in the environment.

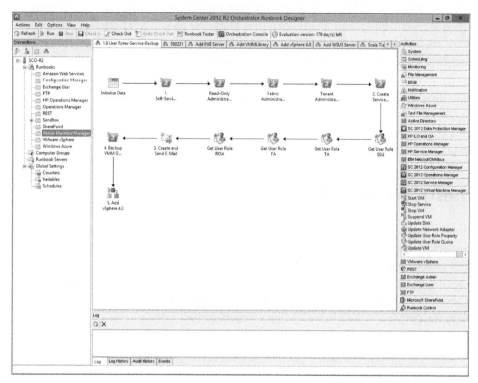

FIGURE 9-2 An example of a runbook that automates a process relating to VMware vSphere.

Figure 9-3 shows the Orchestrator Runbook Designer with the Runbooks workspace selected. In this screen shot, the administrator is reviewing a workflow that integrates System Center 2012 R2 Operations Manager (SCOM) with email and platform events. In this workflow, after several SCOM alerts appear on a server, the server is placed into maintenance mode. If problems continue, an email alert will be sent to an administrator and information will be written to the platform event log.

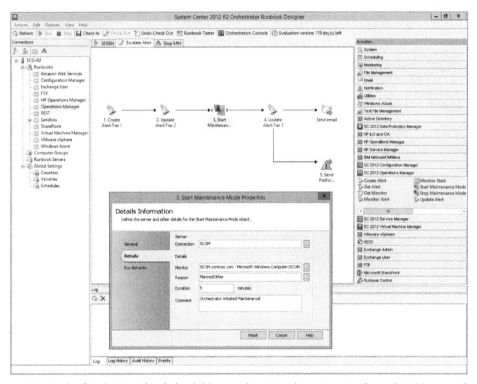

FIGURE 9-3 Configuring a runbook that initiates maintenance in response to Operations Manager alerts.

Figure 9-4 shows the Orchestrator Runbook Designer with the Runbook Tester selected. The Runbook Tester is a utility to verify that the runbook behaves as expected by inputting test parameters and then individually stepping through the different activities. In this screen shot, the administrator is testing an automated deployment of a cloud service in Windows Azure.

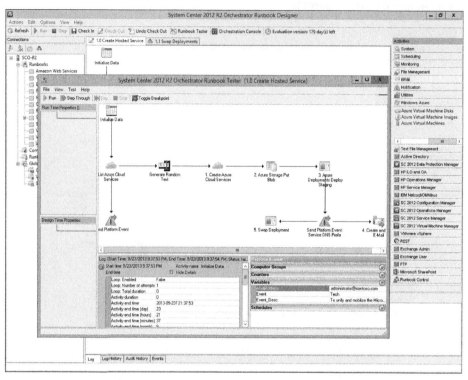

FIGURE 9-4 Testing a runbook before using it in production.

Figure 9-5 shows the Orchestration console with the Runbooks workspace selected. The Orchestration console is a web-based interface that is used to view the health of the Orchestrator tasks across the datacenter. In this screen shot, the administrator is reviewing the details of an Operations Manager runbook.

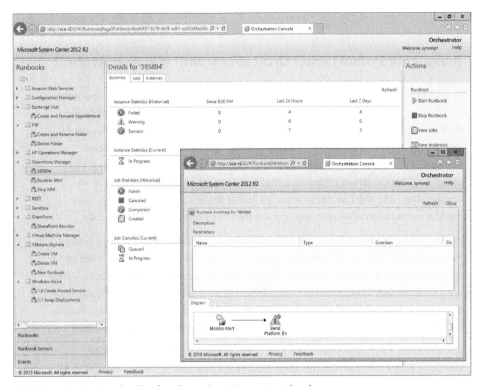

FIGURE 9-5 Reviewing details of an Operations Manager runbook.

Insights from the experts

We'll conclude this chapter by hearing from one of our experts at Microsoft, who shows how you can use the Windows Azure Integration Pack to connect Orchestrator with Windows Azure.

Integrating System Center Orchestrator with Windows Azure

Many people are aware that System Center 2012 is Microsoft's heterogeneous management solution for the datacenter and the desktop, and with Service Pack 1 it also brought many management capabilities that utilize Windows Azure. While System Center consists of a number of components, the major process automation component is System Center Orchestrator, which can be thought of as an IT process automation toolbox that can connect to every IT system in an organization, and then perform activities across those connected systems. This enables automation of almost any process that has a programmatic interface.

While System Center Orchestrator has a number of built-in activity groups related to areas such as File Management, Monitoring, Scheduling, and generic types of communication, it is also possible to download and import integration packs, which are packaged sets of activities and connection types that relate to a particular type of action or solution. A new integration pack that was made available in the System Center 2012 Service Pack 1 timeframe was the Windows Azure Integration Pack.

The Windows Azure Integration Pack not only enables rich interaction with Windows Azure services but also takes advantage of a new System Center 2012 SP1 Orchestrator feature known as *cascading dependencies*, which reduces the number of activities that have to be navigated, while actually making the interaction far more intuitive and adaptive to the exact task you are doing. For example, if a user choses his location as "Europe," a list of Azure datacenters closest to that location are displayed. Download and install the Windows Azure Integration Pack, which is available from *http://technet.microsoft.com/en-us/library/jj721956.aspx*, and deploy it to your Runbook Servers and Runbook Designers.

Connecting Orchestrator to Windows Azure

Windows Azure uses management certificates to allow secure external communication, and System Center 2012 R2 Orchestrator follows this same configuration. First you need to create a custom management certificate and upload it to Windows Azure:

1. Download the Windows SDK and install it from *http://msdn.microsoft.com/en-us/library/windows/desktop/hh852363.aspx*.

2. Run the makecert.exe utility, which is found in the C:\Program Files (x86)\Microsoft SDKs\Windows\v7.1A\Bin\x64 folder, for example:

   ```
   makecert -sk AzureMng -r -n "CN=AzureMng" -pe -a sha1 -len 2048 -ss My
   "AzureMng.cer"
   ```

3. Running the preceding command will create a .CER file that contains the public key of the created certificate. The .CER file must be imported into Windows Azure via the Settings - Management Certificates - Upload option in the Windows Azure Management Portal.

4. The private key created by the makecert command was stored in the user's personal certificate store in the Personal - Certificates location. Use the Certificates MMC snap-in to export the created private key to a .PFX file, and make note of the password you specify during the export. This is covered in detail at *http://windowsitpro.com/system-center/q-how-do-i-create-certificate-enable-system-center-app-controller-manage-windows-azure*.

5. Launch the System Center Orchestrator Runbook Designer.

6. As long as the Windows Azure Integration Pack has been deployed to the Runbook Designer, a Windows Azure Integration Pack will be available in the Activities pane. From the Options menu, select Windows Azure and click the Add button to add a new Windows Azure subscription to manage.

7. Enter a name for the new configuration, and select a type of Azure Management Configuration Settings. Enter the password for the PFX file, specify the location of the exported .PFX file, and enter the Subscription ID of the Windows Azure subscription (which can be found on the Windows Azure management portal) as shown next, and then click OK.

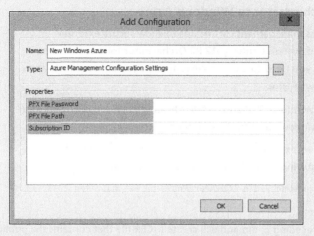

The next step is to actually use the new configuration for Windows Azure to perform tasks in Windows Azure.

Creating a simple virtual machine in Windows Azure using System Center Orchestrator

In this section, a new runbook will be created that creates a new cloud service, storage account, and storage container into which a new virtual machine will be created. Three of the Windows Azure activities will be used:

- **Azure Cloud Services**   Used to create the new cloud service
- **Azure Storage**   Used to create the new storage account and the new storage container
- **Azure Virtual Machines**   Used to create a new virtual machine

Here are the steps in the procedure:

1. Create a new runbook, and then drag the Azure Cloud Services activity onto the canvas and double click it. The activity looks empty.

2. Click the ellipsis (...) for the Configuration Name, and select the Windows Azure configuration previously created. This will enable an activity to be selected.

3. Select Create Cloud Service. This will allow you to select the unique DNS for the service as well as a label, description, and location/affinity group. The following screen shots show the progression of available options that are dynamically generated by the cascading dependency feature of Orchestrator:

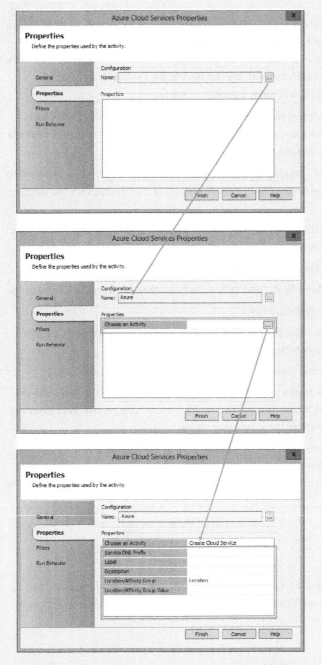

4. Continue by adding the Azure Storage activity with the activity type configured to Create Storage Account, and then specify a name, label, and location. Also set Wait For Completion to True. Make sure the name is lowercase and numeric only. As each activity is added, create the link to connect the entire flow.

5. Add another Azure Storage activity with the activity type configured to Create Container. For the Storage Account Name, use the name from the previous activity (you can even subscribe to the Storage Account Name from the Create Storage Account activity using the databus to pass variables between the different activities), and enter a container name.

6. Add the Azure Virtual Machines activity, and set the activity to Create VM Deployment. There are a lot of options when creating a VM; however, next are some of the key ones to specify:

   - **Service Name**   This is the name created in the first activity. Use Service DNS Prefix from the Create Cloud Service activity on the databus for the simplest option.

   - **Deployment Name, Label, VM Instance Name, and Computer Name**   Set this to a unique name within the service, such as W12R2VM1.

   - **Deployment Slot**   Production.

   - **Use Default Template**   True (allows built-in standard templates to be used).

   - **Image Type**   PlatformImage.

   - **Container URI**   Use the Container URL from the Create Storage Container activity on the databus.

   - **Blob VHD Name**   Select a name for the new virtual hard disk (VHD).

   - **Source Image Name**   Press the ellipsis (...) to see a list of available images and select one. Make sure the Operating System Type property matches the operating system of the image you chose.

   Make sure you complete all other fields, such as Admin Password.

That's everything. You can now run the runbook and create a VM running in your Windows Azure subscription. Here is what your very basic runbook should look like:

In a production runbook, you should have error checking and might divide this up into multiple runbooks. The activities were renamed to make it clearer what each activity is doing.

John Savill
Technology Solutions Professional, Microsoft Technology Center (MTC) Dallas

How to learn more

The following sections provide links where you can learn more about Orchestrator.

Product home page

Your starting point for exploring, trying, buying, deploying, and supporting Orchestrator and other System Center 2012 R2 components is the System Center 2012 R2 home page on Microsoft's Server and Cloud Platform site at *http://www.microsoft.com/en-us/server-cloud/ products/system-center-2012-r2/*.

TechNet Library

If you're already familiar with previous versions of Orchestrator, you might want to start with "What's New in System Center 2012 R2 Orchestrator," found at *http://technet.microsoft.com/ en-us/library/dn251064.aspx*. If you're new to Orchestrator, you can browse the full online documentation for Orchestrator starting from *http://technet.microsoft.com/en-us/library/ hh237242.aspx*. For a list of currently available integration packs for Orchestrator, see *http://technet.microsoft.com/en-us/library/hh295851.aspx*.

Microsoft Download Center

You can download the Orchestrator Integration Toolkit and other add-ons and extensions for System Center 2012 R2 Orchestrator from *http://www.microsoft.com/en-us/download/details .aspx?id=39622*.

TechNet blogs

For the latest information about Orchestrator, follow the System Center Orchestrator Engineering Blog at *http://blogs.technet.com/b/orchestrator/*.

TechNet wiki

The Orchestrator wiki articles can be found at *http://social.technet.microsoft.com/wiki/ contents/articles/703.wiki-management-portal.aspx#System_Center_Opalis_Orchestrator*. See especially the Orchestrator Survival Guide at *http://social.technet.microsoft.com/wiki/contents/ articles/11414.system-center-2012-orchestrator-survival-guide.aspx*.

TechNet forums

To get answers to your questions about Orchestrator, try posting to one of the Orchestrator forums on TechNet at *http://social.technet.microsoft.com/Forums/en-US/home?category=system centerorchestrator*.

TechNet Evaluation Center

You can download evaluation versions of Orchestrator and other System Center 2012 R2 components from the TechNet Evaluation Center at *http://technet.microsoft.com/en-US/evalcenter/dn205295*.

TechNet Virtual Labs

You can try out System Center 2012 R2 products online using the TechNet Virtual Labs at *http://technet.microsoft.com/en-us/virtuallabs*.

Channel 9

Channel 9 on MSDN has lots of helpful videos on Orchestrator. See *http://channel9.msdn.com/search?term=Orchestrator&type=All*.

Microsoft Virtual Academy

The Microsoft Virtual Academy has numerous online courses on Service Manager and other System Center 2012 R2 products at *http://www.microsoftvirtualacademy.com/product-training/system-center*.

Twitter

@SystemCenter is your official Twitter source for System Center solutions and news. You can find reviews, discussions, and helpful information at *https://twitter.com/system_center*.

CHAPTER 10

Windows Azure Pack

This chapter provides a brief overview of Windows Azure Pack for Windows Server. The topics covered in this chapter include

- Introduction to Windows Azure Pack
- Windows Azure Pack in action
- Insights from the experts
- How to learn more

Introduction to Windows Azure Pack

We've saved the best until last. Windows Azure Pack enables you to implement the Windows Azure experience right inside your own datacenter. It's a set of technologies you install and run on top of Windows Server 2012 R2 and System Center 2012 R2 that lets you build a multitenant private cloud with self-service capabilities for provisioning and managing instances of Web Sites, Virtual Machines, Service Bus, SQL and MySQL databases, and other Windows Azure–like cloud services in your own datacenter. Best of all, Windows Azure Pack is available to Microsoft customers at no additional cost.

> **MORE INFO** If you're new to Windows Azure concepts and technologies, you should download and read the free ebook *Introducing Windows Azure for IT Professionals* from Microsoft Press at *http://blogs.msdn.com/b/microsoft_press/archive/2013/10/01/ free-ebook-introducing-windows-azure-for-it-professionals.aspx.*

Windows Azure Pack architecture

Windows Azure Pack provides two types of management portals you can use in your environment:

- **Management portal for administrators** A web-based portal you can use for building resource clouds, offering hosting plans to tenants, managing tenant user accounts, generating usage reports, implementing quotas and billing, and automating cloud management processes using runbooks. This portal is intended for those who will be administering Windows Azure Pack in your environment.

- **Management portal for tenants**   A web-based portal similar to the one for administrators but with functionality that targets those who consume cloud services such as departments, divisions, and other internal customers. This portal enables users to provision, configure, manage, and monitor their web applications, virtual machines, and other cloud resources running on Windows Azure Pack.

Implementing Windows Azure Pack

Windows Azure Pack can be implemented in various ways depending on the needs and size of your organization. Deployment options include

- **Express deployment**   This approach installs all Windows Azure Pack required components on a single server. Express deployment should be used only for proof-of-concept testing purposes because the consolidation of so many components could cause performance delays in a production environment.

- **Distributed deployment**   This approach installs Windows Azure Pack required components on up to eight servers in your environment. Distributed deployment can be used in production environments. It provides greater scalability and enables load-balancing.

In addition to choosing your deployment architecture, you can also choose to deploy any or all of the following optional resource providers available in Windows Azure Pack:

- **Web Sites**   This service allows you to offer tenants the ability to request their own high-density, scalable shared Platform as a Service (PaaS) capabilities for running their ASP.NET, PHP, and Node.js web applications. Web Sites includes a customizable web application gallery that includes open source web applications and allows for integration with source control systems for building custom-developed web sites and applications.

- **Virtual Machines**   This service allows you to offer tenants Infrastructure-as-a-Service (IaaS) capabilities for running their Windows and Linux virtual machines. Virtual Machines includes a virtual machine template gallery (with a selection of Windows Server and Linux distributions), various scaling options, and virtual networking capabilities.

- **Networks**   This service allows you to offer tenants their own private virtual networks, which can be fully isolated or connected to other logical networks. This enables users to connect their virtual machines (VMs) together, create guest clusters, or test new applications that could cause conflicts with infrastructure servers on the production networks.

- **Service Bus**   This service allows you to offer tenants reliable messaging services to connect the different components of their distributed applications. Service Bus includes queued and topic-based publish/subscribe capabilities and supports a variety of standard messaging protocols.

- **SQL and MySQL**   This service allows you to offer tenants dedicated database instances for their web applications hosted on the Web Sites service.
- **Automation and extensibility**   These capabilities allow administrators to implement automation by integrating additional custom services, such as a runbook editor and execution environment, into the Windows Azure Pack services framework, known as Service Manager Automation (SMA). A Windows Azure Pack runbook is designed to automate Windows PowerShell workflows. A comparison between SMA and System Center Orchestrator can be found in the "Insights from the experts" section later in this chapter.

Windows Azure Pack in action

Let's now look at a few examples of Windows Azure Pack in action. Figure 10-1 shows Windows Azure Pack with the My Account workspace selected. This workspace allows the user to subscribe to different service plans. In this screen shot, the self-service user is reviewing all the different service offerings, including Web Sites, Virtual Machines, Networks, Service Bus, SQL Server Databases, and MySQL Databases.

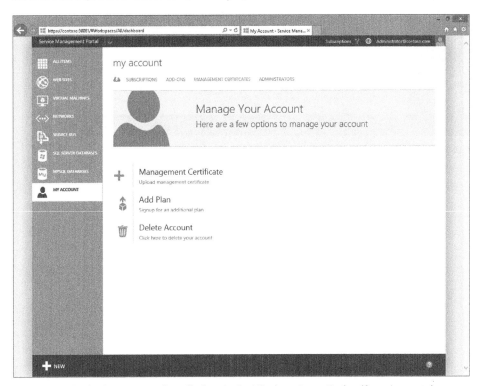

FIGURE 10-1 Reviewing your service offerings in the Windows Azure Pack self-service portal

Figure 10-2 shows Windows Azure Pack with the Web Sites workspace selected. This workspace is used configure websites from a gallery of images. In this screen shot, the end user is preconfiguring the .NET and PHP versions, architecture, websockets, certificates, and more so that these services are already working as soon as the website is provisioned.

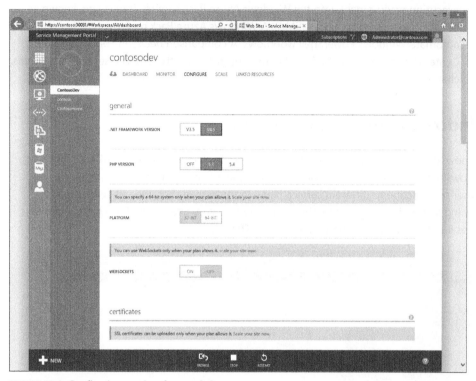

FIGURE 10-2 Configuring services for a website

Figure 10-3 shows Windows Azure Pack with the Virtual Machines workspace selected. This workspace is used to configure Hyper-V Virtual Machines from a gallery of images. In this screen shot, the end user is configuring the VM to use a SQL Server 2012 .VHDX file and providing different hardware and software settings.

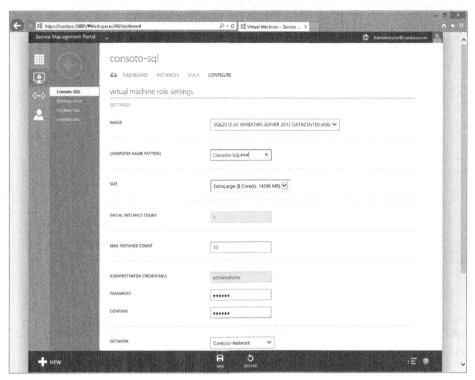

FIGURE 10-3 Configuring the settings for a virtual machine

Figure 10-4 shows Windows Azure Pack with the Virtual Machines workspace selected. In this screen shot, the end user is viewing the resources his VM is consuming.

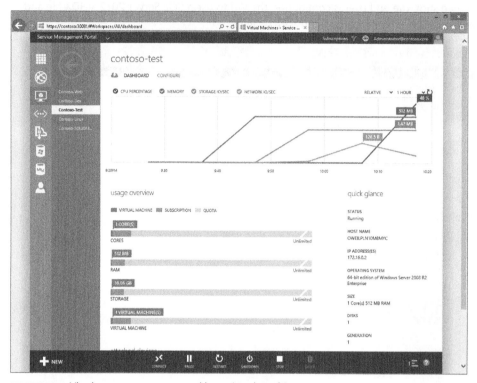

FIGURE 10-4 Viewing resources consumed by a virtual machine

Figure 10-5 shows Windows Azure Pack with the Virtual Machines workspace selected. In this screen shot, the end user is browsing from a gallery of preconfigured Web App images.

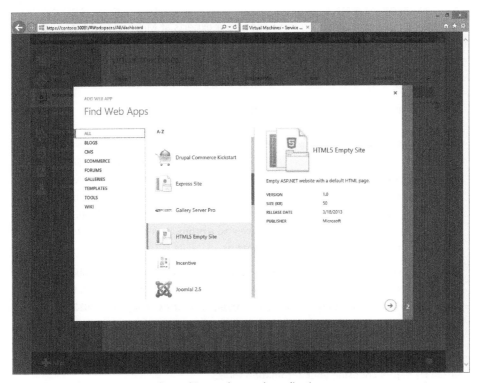

FIGURE 10-5 Choosing a preconfigured image for a web application

Insights from the experts

We'll conclude this chapter by hearing from one of our experts at Microsoft, who provides us with an in-depth look at Service Management Automation (SMA), a new workflow management solution for Windows Azure Pack.

Working with Service Management Automation

SMA is a set of tools for Windows Azure Pack that enables you to automate the creation, monitoring, and deployment of resources in your environment. SMA can be installed from the System Center 2012 R2 Orchestrator installation software and allows you to run Windows PowerShell, workflow-based runbooks that support parallel execution, sequential execution, interruptible jobs, and state tracking. That's a lot of powerful features to introduce into a product, and it brings us to the next levels of automation in cloud environments.

SMA is made of several components, including a web service endpoint, a runbook worker server, a Windows PowerShell module, and a database. You can install the SMA web service and up to three runbook workers from the Orchestrator 2012 R2 Setup program, and an Orchestrator installation is not required in order to have SMA in your environment. Remember, however, that SMA does not replace Orchestrator either. You need to carefully consider the elements you want to automate before choosing your automation tools.

SMA is mainly intended to be accessed via the Windows Azure Pack portal. Within the Windows Azure Pack interface is a GUI representation of the SMA service where you can build, import, and run runbooks. For now, however, don't worry too much about the similarity of the terminology between SMA and Orchestrator, as it might just get a little confusing!

SMA is a web-based service that connects to a SQL database and stores its configuration details and runbooks in an SQL database. It also stores information on which runbooks to execute using what parameters. When you ask a runbook to execute or when you schedule a runbook, SMA becomes a job and is entered into a job table in the SQL database that the runbook worker servers poll and execute whenever a job is present.

Although it is much easier to work with SMA via the Windows Azure Pack, you can also utilize the Windows PowerShell module to perform the same functions. And in some cases you can do this only via the Windows PowerShell module—for example, if you want to deploy more than one runbook worker server.

Let's clarify one bit of terminology before moving forward. I mentioned SMA uses runbooks for automating tasks, but these runbooks are different than Orchestrator runbooks. For example, Orchestrator runbooks are visual, as shown here:

Each item in an Orchestrator runbook is an activity and generally has some small fields you need to configure with input parameters and output data. However, you don't really have to understand the logic behind these activities because they are precompiled pieces of code.

The runbooks in SMA, on the other hand, are Windows PowerShell workflows, which are a collection of cmdlets. Here is a sample runbook you can use with SMA:

```
1    Workflow HelloWorld
2    {
3
4        "Hello World"
5    }
```

```
PS C:\windows\system32> Workflow HelloWorld
{

    "Hello World"
}

PS C:\windows\system32> Helloworld
Hello World

PS C:\windows\system32>
```

A brief introduction to Windows PowerShell workflows

As you can see in the preceding screen shot, the workflow we have created is fairly basic. A key thing you might have noticed is that it looks like a Windows PowerShell function, but it is not! Workflows include several features that require you to author the script a little differently, and the main reason for these differences is that they actually don't execute under Windows PowerShell—they execute instead under Windows Workflow. This means that the code you write for your workflow gets translated to XAML and then runs under Windows Workflow.

Let's introduce a couple of simple concepts that are directly related to SMA to help you move forward.

First let's lay down some simple rules concerning workflows:

- You can't use aliases, which are references to other cmdlets, files, scripts, and so on.
- You need to use the full argument name—that is, you cannot use short argument names.

Let's look at an example of creating a workflow in order to better understand how they work.

Problem: We need to gather information about the BIOS versions deployed on our servers. The information we need includes Manufacturer, Release Date, and SMBiosVersion. Once we gather this information, we can use it to determine if we need to perform a BIOS update on any of our servers.

Solution: To begin, we first need to create our workflow by using the keyword "workflow" followed by a functional name and the curly brackets that will encapsulate our code:

```
Workflow DetectBios { }
```

Next, we need an input parameter that will ask for the name of the server we want to gather BIOS information from. We need to use the *param* keyword to gather such input. Our workflow now becomes the following:

```
Workflow DetectBios{
    Param([string]$srvname) }
```

You can see that we have defined the input variable *$srvname* and typecast it as a string.

The next thing we need to do is introduce some logic to gather the BIOS information from the server. Traditionally, we would have used the following code to do this:

```
Gwmi Win32_Bios
```

or more specifically:

```
gwmi -computername Server01 -class Win32_Bios
```

Remember, however, that you cannot use aliases in workflows. So instead of using the alias *gwmi* for this purpose, we have to use the full version of the cmdlet—namely, *get-wmiobject*. Also, in workflows you cannot specify the *–computername* argument. Finally, we need to run *get-wmiobject* in a special way. Specifically, to execute the command correctly within a workflow, we have to use something called *InlineScript*, which allows standard Windows PowerShell commands to execute in a normal way and then return the data to the workflow.

In our sample workflow, our code now becomes the following:

```
Workflow DetectBios{
Param([string]$srvname)
$biosinfo=InLineScript{ Get-Wmiobject –Class Win32_Bios | Select
    Manufacturer,SerialNumber,releaseDate,SMBIOSBIOSVersion }
    -pscomputername $server
$biosinfo
 }
```

We included the *$biosinfo* variable on the second last line to provide output for the command so that when you run the workflow it will output something into the console. We also used the *–pscomputername* argument. This is similar to using the *–computername* argument if you run *get-wmiobject* normally, and it simply means that the cmdlet specified in the InlineScript section of the code will get executed directly on the target server.

If you run this workflow directly from Windows PowerShell using an account that has permissions to query BIOS information on the remote server, some information will be returned. It is important to ensure that the service accounts for the runbook server have the necessary privileges on remote servers to query such information.

A powerful feature of SMA is the ability to create resources for later use by other SMA runbooks. These resources can include Windows PowerShell modules, variables, schedules, credentials, and connections. Here, we're going to call the stored credentials and use them in the workflow. Later in this section, we'll show you how to create resources when you are in the Windows Azure Pack portal.

You can call resources in a workflow by using one of several Get-Automation* cmdlets. In this case, we'll use the *Get-AutomationPSCredential* cmdlet, which requires that you know the name of the resource you are calling. Our sample workflow now becomes this:

```
Workflow DetectBios{
Param([string]$srvname)
$Credentials = Get-AutomationPSCredential –Name "Admin"
$biosinfo=InLineScript{ Get-Wmiobject –Class Win32_Bios | Select
    Manufacturer,SerialNumber,releaseDate,SMBIOSBIOSVersion }
    -psComputerName $server –psCredential $Credentials
$biosinfo
 }
```

Our workflow will now execute under the specified Admin account so that it can retrieve the BIOS information we requested.

But let's say we wanted to change the Windows Management Instrumentation (WMI) class we wanted to query for. Now our workflow really becomes a tool for

IT administrators because it makes it really easy to query lots of WMI information. Here, we changed the workflow name and the variables used. The main thing to realize from this script is the use of the variable *$using:wmiclass* inside the InlineScript. Because the InlineScript activity runs Windows PowerShell commands in a workflow, we need to tell it to use our variable *wmiclass* by using the *$using* variable.

Our script now looks like this:

```
Workflow WMIClassQuery{
Param([string]$srvname,[string]$wmiclass)
$Credentials = Get-AutomationPSCredential -Name "Admin"
$wmiinfo=InLineScript{ Get-Wmiobject -Class $Using:wmiclass }
   -psComputerName $server -psCredential $Credentials
$wmiinfo
 }
```

Let's save the code for the DetectBios workflow as *DetectBios.ps1* because we'll be using it later on.

SMA with Windows Azure Pack

The Windows Azure Pack (WAP) is a front-end web portal that provides access in order to request services (such as virtual machines, web sites, SQL servers, and so on). If you have used Windows Azure services before (*http://www.windowsazure.com*), you will notice that the Windows Azure Pack portal looks almost exactly the same, except it is missing several services that are only offered in Azure. Here is what the Windows Azure Pack portal looks like:

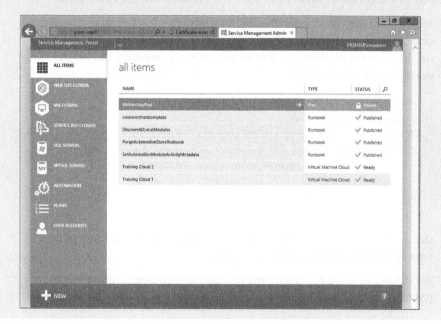

You can see on the left side that there are many options you can configure and provision for tenants to request services for. This is good, but here we will be focusing on automation. Automation in this case is the web GUI for SMA. The first thing you need to do is register your SMA endpoint. Here is what the Automation section of the Windows Azure Pack portal looks like with the SMA endpoint registered:

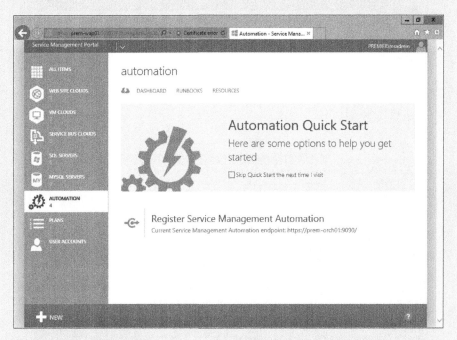

In the preceding screen shot, you can see three pages you can select from: Dashboard, Runbooks, and Resources. Dashboard will give you a summary of what has happened in relation to automation. This is useful for a quick look to see if you have lots of jobs failing or a large number of runbooks executing that you were not expecting. But the two views we are most interested in here are Runbooks and Resources.

The next screen shot shows an example of the Runbooks page. The first thing to notice here is that you can filter by Job Status, allowing you to get a clear picture of what works and what doesn't. In the lower half of the page, you can see four runbooks that are already in place, together with information about their status:

The bottom bar shows the options that are available for the runbooks. By using the New button, you can create a new runbook in the portal:

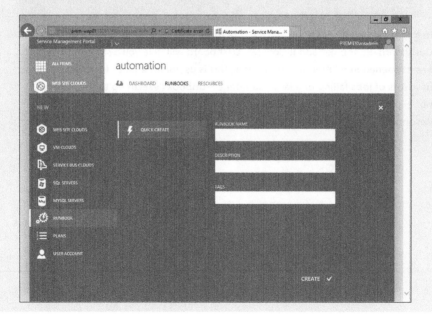

You can simply enter the information necessary and click Create to generate a basic runbook that has the initial Workflow *name* {} element you desire.

Because we already created a runbook earlier and saved it as the DetectBios.ps1 file, let's now import it into SMA via WAP. Windows Azure Pack does some basic error checking to ensure the workflow is in the right format for a runbook, and then a new runbook called *detectbios* is created.

All runbooks are assigned the Draft status when they are first imported. This allows you to test the runbook; then, once you are satisfied, you can publish the runbook for wider use by other tenants. To view the properties of the runbook, you just click on the runbook name or click the arrow that appears when you hover the cursor over the name of the runbook.

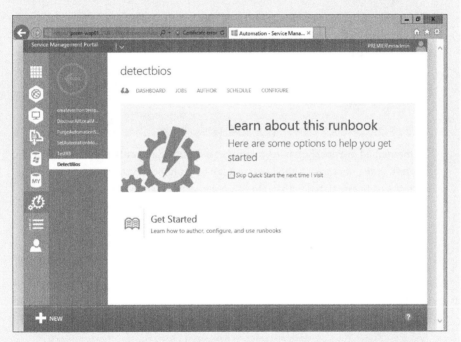

Because we have not yet run this runbook, there will be nothing in the Dashboard or Jobs page worth noting. With this in mind, the first page worth examining is Author, as shown in the screen shot on the following page. As you can see, there are two possible states that a runbook can be in: Draft and Published. These are similar to the Checked In/Checked Out states in Orchestrator:

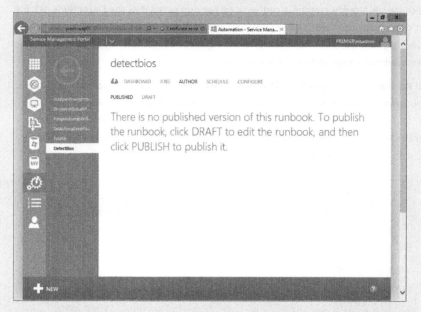

As mentioned previously, when you import a runbook, the default state it will be in is Draft. In the next screen shot, you can see our runbook in the Draft state together with the code associated with it. On this page, you can edit your workflow if you need to make changes during your testing:

At the bottom of the screen, there are some new options to examine. The Manage button allows you to either import a custom Windows PowerShell module you are dependent on or create a setting (which are stored under Resources), such as a new set of credentials or a new connection. Insert allows you to select settings you already configured and inject them into the workflow code.

In our case, we already created the workflow and referenced Admin credentials in it, but because we have not yet created our Admin credentials, if we test our runbook now it will fail. We can do this by using the Manage button and then selecting Add Setting.

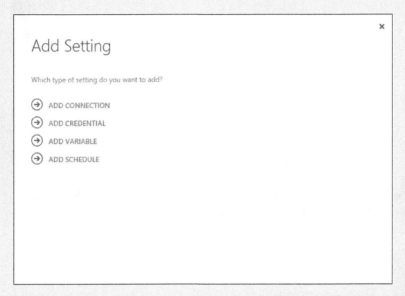

We will choose the Add Credential option. This brings us to the Define Credential dialog box shown on the following page, where we choose which type of credentials we want to store. We have the choices here of selecting either

PowerShell Credential or Certificates. In our case, we need to choose PowerShell Credential. The Name field should show the name we already referenced in our runbook—namely, Administrator:

Next we need to specify the username and password for the credentials. Because there is no field for specifying the domain, you have to ensure the username is in the format *domain\username*:

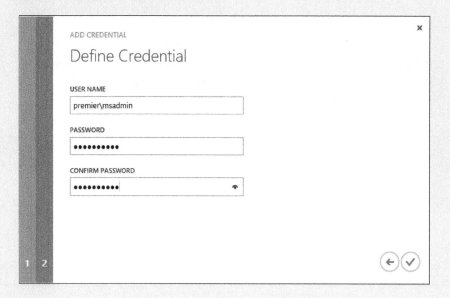

Now let's perform a test of our runbook. We can do this by pressing Test on the bottom menu. Attempting to start the runbook causes it to notice the param line, which is asking for input. This displays a screen asking for the input variable—in this case, SRVNAME. When the runbook has completed its run, it will display in the output pane on the same screen, as shown here:

You can click View Details on the bottom menu to view the output of the runbook you just tested:

The final step is to publish our runbook now that we have verified its operation. To do this, click the Publish button on the bottom menu. You will be asked if you are sure whether you want to save and publish your runbook. The runbook will now switch from Draft and Published, and you will no longer be able to edit its code. If you click back on the Draft page, however, you will get an option to edit the code and it will unpublish your runbook and return it to its Draft state.

If you now click on Dashboard, you will see a Start button on the bottom menu:

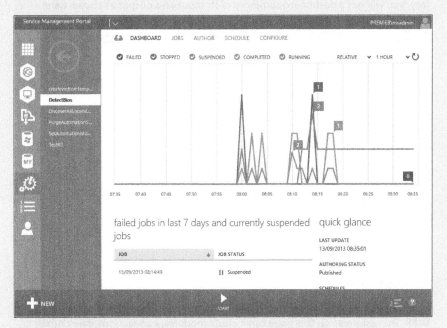

Click the Start button. As in the test run, the runbook will prompt you for SRVNAME. Once you have supplied this information, the runbook will execute and you will be able to view the results on the Jobs page:

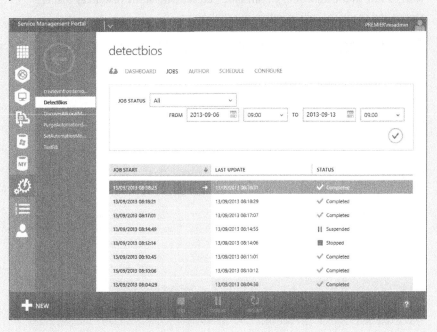

If you double-click on the last job run (which in this walkthrough is the DetectBios job), you will get a dashboard summary of its input and output as shown here:

Finally, let's also take a look at the Resources page of the Automation section of WAP. The resources on this page can include modules, connections, credentials, and so on. The procedure for creating any of these resources is exactly as described earlier: just use the Add Setting button and choose the appropriate resource you wish to add. In the following screen shot, you can see all the resources that are stored and ready for calling within our runbooks:

SMA with Windows PowerShell

Now that we understand how the Windows Azure Pack portal works with SMA, let's see how to work with SMA without using the Windows Azure Pack portal. SMA can be managed in this way entirely using Windows PowerShell.

First let's see what commands are available for doing this via Windows PowerShell. The name of the Windows PowerShell module for SMA is Microsoft.SystemCenter. ServiceManagementAutomation. If we want to see all the cmdlets available to use in this module, we can do this using the following syntax:

```
get-command –module Microsoft.SystemCenter.ServiceManagementAutomation
```

Here is the output from this command, which lists all available cmdlets for SMA:

Let's now take a closer look at some of these cmdlets:

- Get-SmaCredential
- Set-SmaCredential
- Get-SmaRunbook
- Start-SmaRunbook
- Get-SmaJob
- Get-SmaJobOutput
- Import-SmaRunbook
- Edit-SmaRunbook
- Publish-SmaRunbook

Each of these cmdlets when executed will want to know the WebServiceEndpoint, which is the SMA web service that has been previously deployed. The SMA web service installs by default to port 9090. The cmdlet automatically assumes this port, so you can just specify the basic URL like https://server01 and it will automatically connect to port 9090.

The first cmdlet we will look at is Get-SmaCredential. The syntax to run it is as follows:

```
Get-SmaCredential -WebServiceEndpoint https://server01
```

Some output from running this command is shown here:

You can see some credential information for the Administrator and Admin accounts we previously set up in WAP.

If you want to create a new set of credentials, you can use Set-SmaCredential. The following syntax can be used:

```
Set-SmaCredential -WebServiceEndpoint https://server01
    -name "MyAdminCreds" -value (get-credential)
```

Using this command will create a new set of credentials that you can then call by using MyAdminCreds. Here is some output for this command:

Next, let's see which runbooks are available on our SMA installation. Because we already created a few runbooks from our Windows Azure Pack portal, we should be able to detect our DetectBios runbook. The syntax is as follows:

```
Get-SmaRunbook -WebServiceEndpoint https://server01
    -Runbookname DetectBios
```

Some things to notice in the output shown next are *PublishedRunBookVersionID* and *DraftRunbookVersionID*, which you can use to determine whether the runbook is draft or published:

```
PS C:\Users\msadmin> Get-SmaRunbook -WebServiceEndpoint https://prem-orch01 -RunbookName DetectBios

TenantID                 : 00000000-0000-0000-0000-000000000000
RunbookID                : 91d54d2c-3b02-4638-acbc-2f5f16b7514a
RunbookName              : DetectBios
CreationTime             : 13/09/2013 04:36:40
LastModifiedTime         : 13/09/2013 07:35:01
Description              :
IsApiOnly                : False
IsGlobal                 : False
PublishedRunbookVersionID : 0f1831a4-dbae-4e49-9d3b-fae50d45ebf2
DraftRunbookVersionID    :
Tags                     :
LogDebug                 : False
LogVerbose               : False
LogProgress              : False
Statistics               :
DraftRunbookVersion      :
PublishedRunbookVersion  :
Schedules                : {}

PS C:\Users\msadmin>
```

Let's now invoke this particular runbook by using the Start-SmaRunbook cmdlet. First, we need to capture the RunbookID using the following syntax:

```
$runbookid = (Get-SmaRunbook -WebServiceEndpoint https://server01
    -Runbookname DetectBios).Runbookid
```

Now we can use the captured RunbookID in the following syntax:

```
$jobid = Start-SmaRunbook -WebServiceEndpoint https://server01
    -Runbookid $runbookid -parameters @{"SRVNAME="SERVER02"}
```

Here, we stored the job in a variable named *$jobid*, so we can query the job later and use this information. We also used a hash table to specify the input parameters for our runbook. Because we have a single input parameter named *$srvname*, in the hash table we do not specify the *$*.

Next we will query the job using the Get-SmaJob cmdlet, which has the following syntax:

```
Get-SmaJob -WebServiceEndpoint https://server01 -jobid $jobid
```

The output is shown here:

```
PS C:\Users\msadmin> get-smajob -webserviceendpoint https://prem-orch01 -JobId $jobid

JobId             : a3d84a1c-4bc2-43b9-a202-6a4e903719cd
JobContextId      : 216b0a36-de65-4e58-99a2-cb2982665a30
RunbookId         : 91d54d2c-3b02-4638-acbc-2f5f16b7514a
TenantId          : 00000000-0000-0000-0000-000000000000
JobStatus         : Completed
StartTime         : 13/09/2013 08:46:51
EndTime           : 13/09/2013 08:46:52
CreationTime      : 13/09/2013 08:46:45
LastModifiedTime  : 13/09/2013 08:46:52
ErrorCount        : 0
WarningCount      : 0
JobException      :

PS C:\Users\msadmin>
```

Because the job has completed, we will review its output to ensure it's the same as what we got in the Windows Azure Pack portal. To do this, we can use the Get-SmaJobOutput cmdlet with the following syntax:

```
Get-SmaJobOutput –webserviceendpoint https://server01 –jobid $jobid
    –outputtype Output
```

There are many options you can choose from for *OutputType*, such as the following:

- Any
- Error
- Output
- Progress
- Warning

In the next screen shot, we show that the output of the job is very similar in Windows PowerShell to what we observed previously in the Windows Azure Pack portal:

The last set of cmdlets we want to examine are those for importing a runbook, publishing it, and turning it back to draft for further editing. We will use this example again:

```
Workflow WMIClassQuery{
Param([string]$srvname,[string]$wmiclass)
$Credentials = Get-AutomationPSCredential -Name "Admin"
$wmiinfo=InLineScript{ Get-Wmiobject –Class $Using:wmiclass }
    -psComputerName $server –psCredential $Credentials
$wmiinfo
    }
```

Let's now save this as a .ps1 file named *WMIClassQuery.ps1* in a folder named *c:\scripts*. Now let's import the workflow we just saved as a runbook by using the following syntax:

```
$runbook = Import-SmaRunbook –Runbookpath c:\scripts\WmiClassQuery.ps1
    -WebServiceEndpoint https://server01
```

Here is some output from running Import-SmaRunbook:

```
PS C:\scripts> Import-SmaRunbook -RunbookPath "c:\scripts\WMIClassQuery.ps1" -WebServiceEndpoint https://prem-orch01

TenantID         : 00000000-0000-0000-0000-000000000000
RunbookVersionID : dc60f16e-cc76-40f7-96d8-605add5a1cec
RunbookID        : 2c7a48be-b7bd-4870-add4-e0074e79eb32
VersionNumber    : 1
IsDraft          : True
CreationTime     : 13/09/2013 10:16:00
LastModifiedTime : 13/09/2013 10:16:00
JobContexts      : {}
Runbook          :
RunbookParameters : {}


PS C:\scripts>
```

As shown by the previous code sample, we can store the output of the Import-SmaRunbook command in a variable named *$runbook* so that we can use the runbook ID for the next commands.

To publish the runbook so that it can be executed, we use the Publish-SmaRunbook cmdlet. Here is the syntax:

```
Publish-SmaRunbook -WebServiceEndpoint https://server01
    -Runbookid $runbook.runbookid
```

The preceding command changes the runbook status from Draft to Published.

Now let's use the Start-SmaRunbook cmdlet and specify the parameters for SRVNAME and WMICLASS using the following syntax:

```
$jobid = Start-SmaRunbook -Runbook $runbook.runbookid
    -WebServiceEndpoint https://server01
    -parameters @{"SRVNAME"="SERVER01";
    "WMICLASS"="Win32_ComputerSystem"}
```

We wait a few seconds for the job to invoke and complete. Finally, we use the Get-SmaJobOutput cmdlet to display the output of the job:

```
Get-SmaJobOutput -jobid $jobid -WebServiceEndpoint https://server01
    -OutputType Output
```

The output in this example is from calling the Win32_ComputerSystem class, as shown here:

```
PS C:\scripts> Get-SmaJobOutput -JobId $jobid -WebServiceEndpoint https://prem-orch01 -OutputType Output

JobId            : 232dea42-3be3-4b58-8d97-84d191b5ec3d
NameValues       : {PSComputerName, PSShowComputerName, PSSourceJobInstanceId, __GENUS...}
RunbookVersionId : f6be022a-436a-4de9-85c9-a7615543fa3f
StreamTypeName   : Output
TenantId         : 00000000-0000-0000-0000-000000000000
StreamTime       : 13/09/2013 12:57:10
StreamText       :

                    Domain           : premier.local
                    Manufacturer     : Dell Inc.
                    Model            : PowerEdge R610
                    Name             : PREM-TR04
                    PrimaryOwnerName : Windows User
                    TotalPhysicalMemory : 34346192896
                    PSComputerName   : localhost
```

In conclusion, SMA is a powerful product that has huge potential to enhance datacenter automation through self-service. For additional information, see the "Get Started with Service Management Automation: Walkthrough Guide" at *http://technet.microsoft.com/en-us/library/dn296458.aspx*.

John McCabe
Sr. Premier Field Engineer at Microsoft

How to learn more

The following sections provide links where you can learn more about Windows Azure Pack.

Product home page

Your starting point for exploring, trying, buying, deploying, and supporting Windows Azure Pack is this page on Microsoft's Server and Cloud Platform site: *http://www.microsoft.com/en-us/server-cloud/products/windows-azure-pack/default.aspx*.

TechNet Library

Technical information on deploying and administering Windows Azure Pack can be found at *http://technet.microsoft.com/en-us/library/dn296435.aspx*. You can also download technical documentation for Windows Azure Pack from the Microsoft Download Center at *http://www.microsoft.com/en-us/download/details.aspx?id=40792*.

TechNet wiki

The Windows Azure Pack wiki can be found at *http://social.technet.microsoft.com/wiki/contents/articles/20689.wap-wiki-a-collection-of-windows-azure-pack-and-related-blogs-videos-and-technet-articles.aspx*.

TechNet forums

To get answers to your questions about Windows Azure Pack, try posting to one of the Windows Azure Pack forums on TechNet at *http://social.msdn.microsoft.com/Forums/windowsazure/en-US/home?forum=windowsazurepack*.

Channel 9

Channel 9 on MSDN has lots of helpful videos on Windows Azure Pack. See *http://channel9 .msdn.com/search?term=azure+pack&type=All.*

Twitter

@WindowsAzure is your official Twitter source for Windows Azure solutions and news. You can find reviews, discussions, and helpful information at *https://twitter.com/windowsazure.*

Index

C

D

E

Y

About the authors

 MITCH TULLOCH is a well-known expert on Windows Server administration and virtualization. He has published hundreds of articles on a wide variety of technology sites and has written or contributed to over two dozen books, including the *Windows 7 Resource Kit* (Microsoft Press, 2009), for which he was lead author; *Understanding Microsoft Virtualization Solutions: From the Desktop to the Datacenter* (Microsoft Press, 2010); and *Introducing Windows Server 2012* (Microsoft Press, 2012), a free e-book that has been downloaded almost three-quarters of a million times.

Mitch has been repeatedly awarded Most Valuable Professional (MVP) status by Microsoft for his outstanding contributions to supporting the global IT community. He is a nine-time MVP in the technology area of Windows Server Software Packaging, Deployment & Servicing. You can find his MVP Profile page at *http://mvp.microsoft.com/en-us/mvp/Mitch%20Tulloch-21182*.

Mitch is also Senior Editor of WServerNews (*http://www.wservernews.com*), a weekly newsletter focused on system admin and security issues for the Windows Server platform. With more than 100,000 IT Pro subscribers worldwide, WServerNews is the largest Windows Server–focused newsletter in the world.

Mitch runs an IT content-development business based in Winnipeg, Canada that produces white papers and other collateral for the business decision maker (BDM) and technical decision maker (TDM) audiences. His published content ranges from white papers about Microsoft cloud technologies to reviews of third-party products designed for the Windows Server platform. Before starting his own business in 1998, Mitch worked as a Microsoft Certified Trainer (MCT) for Productivity Point. For more information about Mitch, visit his website at *http://www.mtit.com*. You can also follow Mitch on Twitter at *http://twitter.com/mitchtulloch* or like him on Facebook at *http://www.facebook.com/mitchtulloch*.

 SYMON PERRIMAN is Microsoft's Senior Technical Evangelist covering Private Cloud, Virtualization & System Center, and is a recognized industry expert in datacenter management, cloud, virtualization, high-availability, disaster recovery, mobile technologies, and social media. In this corporate position, he serves as a worldwide technical lead for many of Microsoft's IT Professional programs, including TechNet, Microsoft Learning, the Microsoft Virtual Academy, Jump Start events, the Edge Show, TechEd, virtualization compete, and numerous executive engagements. He is also a regular keynote presenter and trainer at Microsoft conferences around the world, and he delivers over a hundred presentations at in-person events and online each year. Previously, he spent four years as a Program Manager on the Server Clustering & High-Availability engineering team and has been working in the technology industry since 2002.

Symon holds several patents and industry certifications, including Microsoft Certified Trainer (MCT), MCSE Private Cloud, and VMware Certified Professional (VCP). In addition to this book, he has contributed to four technical books for Hyper-V virtualization, Failover Clustering, Windows Server, and SQL Server and has had his technologies featured in PC Magazine, Reuters News, and the Wall Street Journal.

Symon also serves as president and founder of FanWide Technologies LLC. FanWide offers a variety of technical services, including domain name management, website design and hosting, mobile development, social media marketing, and trivia services. FanWide celebrated the recent release of its 100th mobile app and is providing technical services for several upcoming network TV shows.

Symon was born in England, where he lived until he was nine, but he grew up in the United States and currently lives in downtown Seattle with his fiancée, Ashley, and their cat, Malibu. He graduated from Duke University with degrees in Computer Science, Economics, and Film & Digital Studies. In his free time, Symon enjoys NFL football, college basketball, foosball, golf, Frisbee, classic art, electronic music, music festivals, camping, traveling, trivia, film, technology, home automation projects, blackjack strategy, juggling, and other circus arts.

For more information about Symon, visit his website at *http://www.SymonPerriman.com*.

You can also connect with Symon on Twitter (*http://twitter.com/SymonPerriman*), Facebook (*http://www.facebook.com/SymonWPerriman*), and LinkedIn (*http://www.linkedin.com/in/symonperriman*), or check out his weekly webcast on the Edge Show at *http://channel9.msdn.com/Shows/Edge*.

Now that you've read the book...

Tell us what you think!

Was it useful?
Did it teach you what you wanted to learn?
Was there room for improvement?

Let us know at http://aka.ms/tellpress

Your feedback goes directly to the staff at Microsoft Press,
and we read every one of your responses. Thanks in advance!

 Microsoft

CPSIA information can be obtained at www.ICGtesting.com
Printed in the USA
LVOW03s1552090114

368761LV00004B/10/P

This Is Your Government™

THE DEPARTMENT OF AGRICULTURE

Maxine Rosaler

rosen
central™

The Rosen Publishing Group, Inc., New York

Published in 2006 by The Rosen Publishing Group, Inc.
29 East 21st Street, New York, NY 10010

Copyright © 2006 by The Rosen Publishing Group, Inc.

First Edition

Library of Congress Cataloging-in-Publication Data

Rosaler, Maxine.
The Department of Agriculture / by Maxine Rosaler.—1st ed.
    p. cm.—(This is your government)
Includes bibliographical references.
Contents: The history of the USDA—The Secretaries of Agriculture—How the
USDA works—The USDA in the twenty-first century.
ISBN 1-4042-0206-4 (lib. bdg.)
ISBN 1-4042-0659-0 (pbk. bdg.)
1. United States. Dept. of Agriculture—Juvenile literature. 2. Agriculture and
state—United States—Juvenile literature. [1. United States. Dept. of
Agriculture.]
I. Title. II. Series.

S21.C9R67 2004
354.5'0973—dc22
                                                                2003027722

Manufactured in the United States of America

On the cover: Secretaries of agriculture, from left to right: Norman Jay
Coleman, Henry Agard Wallace, Ezra Taft Benson, Ann M. Veneman, and
Mike Johanns.

CONTENTS

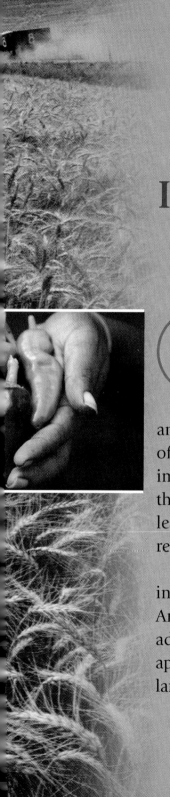

Introduction

The United States is a fortunate country when it comes to the basics of life. It is rich in natural resources, such as water, good soil, coal, natural gas, and timber. These resources help create wealth and provide for the feeding and sheltering of most of the nation's citizens. Food is one of the most important necessities for sustaining life. Thanks to the rich soils of America's heartland and the tireless efforts of its farmers, the nation enjoys a large, reliable, and varied supply of food.

American agriculture is the most productive in the world, thanks to the vast resources of America's land, the skills of its farmers, and the advanced science and technology they are able to apply to civilization's oldest art—the cultivation of land and the raising of crops. Less than 3 percent

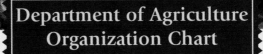

Department of Agriculture Organization Chart

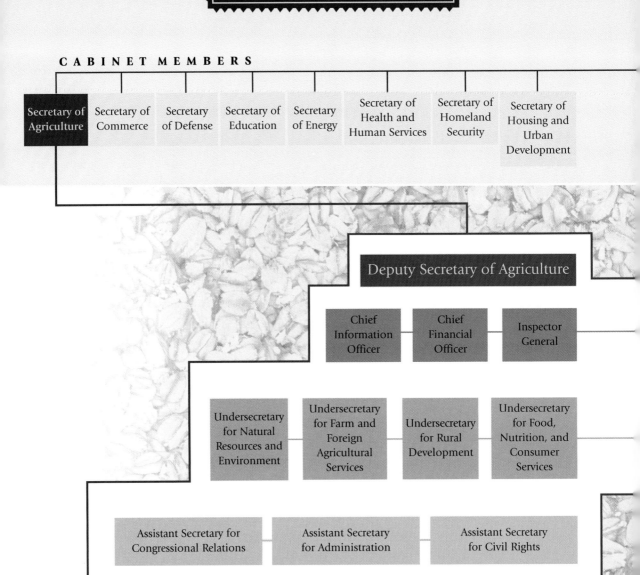

CABINET MEMBERS

- Secretary of Agriculture
- Secretary of Commerce
- Secretary of Defense
- Secretary of Education
- Secretary of Energy
- Secretary of Health and Human Services
- Secretary of Homeland Security
- Secretary of Housing and Urban Development

Deputy Secretary of Agriculture

- Chief Information Officer
- Chief Financial Officer
- Inspector General

- Undersecretary for Natural Resources and Environment
- Undersecretary for Farm and Foreign Agricultural Services
- Undersecretary for Rural Development
- Undersecretary for Food, Nutrition, and Consumer Services

- Assistant Secretary for Congressional Relations
- Assistant Secretary for Administration
- Assistant Secretary for Civil Rights

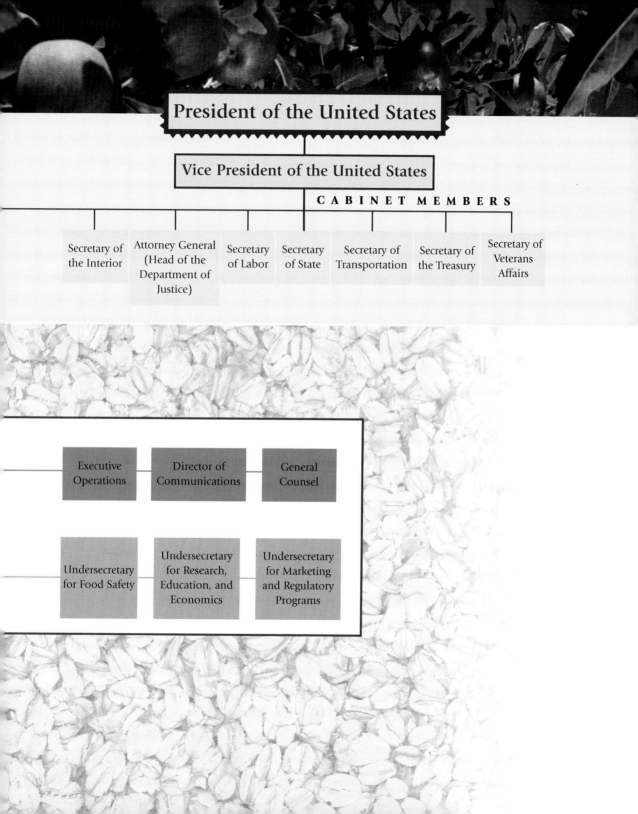

President of the United States

Vice President of the United States

CABINET MEMBERS

Secretary of the Interior	Attorney General (Head of the Department of Justice)	Secretary of Labor	Secretary of State	Secretary of Transportation	Secretary of the Treasury	Secretary of Veterans Affairs

Executive Operations	Director of Communications	General Counsel

Undersecretary for Food Safety	Undersecretary for Research, Education, and Economics	Undersecretary for Marketing and Regulatory Programs

of Americans are full-time farmers, yet they are able to produce more than enough food to feed an entire country of more than a quarter of a billion people. In fact, American farmers produce much more than even their huge country requires. They export vast amounts of food, shipping millions of tons of grain and produce overseas in giant cargo containers. One-third of American farm products are exported. At home, American supermarkets hold an overwhelming assortment of meats, grains, cheeses, fruits, and vegetables.

American agriculture is a remarkably successful industry. Making sure that it remains successful is the job of a federal government agency, the U.S. Department of Agriculture (USDA). The USDA is responsible for the health of the farming business and the safety of the food supply. The person in charge of the department, the secretary of agriculture, has an enormous responsibility to American farmers and to the American and foreign consumers of their products.

The USDA has an annual budget of $63 billion—an amount greater than the total national budget of most countries—and it employs about 109,000 people. Because of the great importance of the USDA, the secretary of agriculture is a cabinet-level position. This means that the secretary is directly appointed by the president of the United States, with the advice and consent, or agreement, of the U.S. Congress. Once appointed, the secretary of agriculture advises the president

A cargo ship is loaded with storage containers that hold American produce heading overseas. The USDA ships several million metric tons of agricultural products each year for international food-aid programs. U.S. commodities, including wheat, corn, soybeans, and rice, are shipped to about fifty countries.

on all agricultural issues. As head of the USDA, the secretary of agriculture also puts the president's decisions concerning the industry into effect.

At first glance, it would seem that the USDA would be one of the few government agencies that attracts little controversy. Its basic purposes and goals—helping farmers and keeping consumers safe and healthy—are hard to argue with, after all. But anything that the government does can be a subject for hot debate, and the activities of the USDA are no exception.

Should U.S. farmers produce genetically modified food (natural products that have been altered by scientists to make them bigger or shinier or longer lasting)? Should such food be labeled so consumers can make an informed choice about whether to buy or avoid it? If twenty people a year die from eating tainted meat and that number could be cut in half by hiring twice as many safety inspectors, should the additional inspectors be hired? How much regulation is needed to protect consumers? How much regulation is too restrictive and costly for farmers and producers? Should farmers be paid not to grow certain crops, in order to keep the supply low enough and the price high enough so that most farmers can make a profit?

Answers to these questions are neither simple nor straight-forward. Not only do they concern farmers and consumers, but they also have a political element. These tough decisions are made by the president and Congress with the advice of the secretary of agriculture. Everyone involved in the decision-making process tries to balance the often competing wants and needs of farmers, farm suppliers, agricultural scientists, food companies, and average consumers whose health is directly affected by what they eat for breakfast, lunch, and dinner.

CHAPTER ONE

The History of the USDA

Agriculture has always been important to the United
States, not only for its crucial role in sustaining the lives
of U.S. citizens but also for its economic value. From its begin-
nings to the present day, the United States has exported
agricultural products, and most American farmers have sold at
least part of their crops to other countries. When the thirteen
American colonies declared their independence from Great
Britain in 1776, farming was the main occupation of more
than three-quarters of the people who lived in what was about
to become the United States.

The idea of creating a national agency to assist American
farmers was first proposed to the Continental Congress by

Virginia delegate George Washington in 1776. The Continental Congress was the new country's first national representative government. Congress did not act on Washington's suggestion at the time, but in several states, farmers formed societies dedicated to agricultural improvement.

The Birth of the Patent Office's Agricultural Division

The federal government—the central government of the United States that has authority over the individual states and is led by the president, Congress, and the Supreme Court—began to pay closer attention to agriculture in the nineteenth century, as the young nation grew in size and complexity. By 1825, both the House of Representatives and the Senate—the lower and upper houses of Congress—had agriculture committees.

It was not until 1839, however, that Congress established a separate agricultural division within the Patent Office. One of the first things that Congress directed this new agricultural division to do was to collect agricultural statistics. The division's annual budget was $1,000, a far cry from the $65 billion budget of today's Department of Agriculture.

The Creation of the Department of Agriculture

By the mid-nineteenth century, some senators and congressmen wanted the department of agriculture to be a cabinet-level department, with a secretary who would be one of the president's

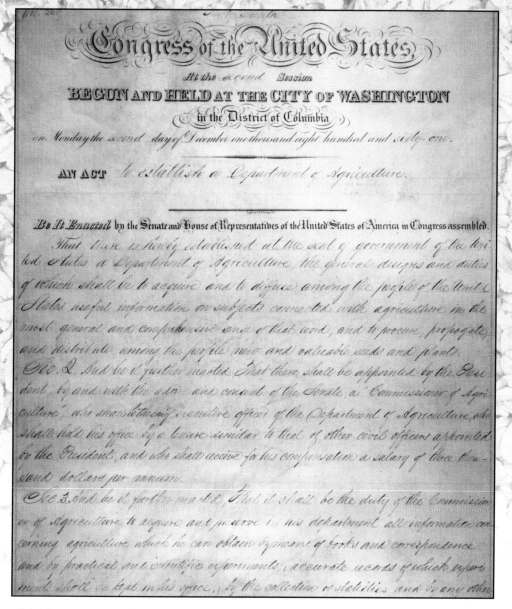

This document is the act that created the United States Department of Agriculture. It was passed by the U.S. Congress on December 2, 1861, and was signed into law by President Abraham Lincoln on May 15, 1862. The USDA would not become a cabinet-level department, however, until 1889.

key advisers—like the secretary of war (who later became the secretary of defense) and the secretary of state. Other lawmakers did not want to give that much power to the department, however, so at its founding in 1862, the Department of Agriculture was made a part of the Department of the Interior. The person in charge of it was called the commissioner of agriculture, rather than the secretary of agriculture.

President Abraham Lincoln signed the bill creating the Agriculture Department on May 15, 1862. The new department would be responsible for acquiring, testing, and distributing new and valuable seeds and plants and conducting scientific experiments. It would also collect agricultural statistics and publish reports that would provide farmers with useful information.

Lincoln called this new department the "people's department," since at that time a larger proportion of Americans earned their living through agriculture than in any other industry or profession. Ninety percent of all Americans earned at least part of their income from the agriculture industry. Full-time farmers made up about 48 percent of the U.S. population when Lincoln was president, down from 75 percent in colonial times.

The Changing Role of the USDA

During its early years, the main purpose of the Department of Agriculture was simply to make American farms more productive.

Scientists in the Department of Agriculture studied diseases in crops and farm animals, as well as the role plant and animal nutrition played in fighting disease and maintaining health. Department scientists also experimented with the ways chemicals could be used to keep insects from damaging crops.

The focus of the USDA began to expand during the 1880s as the processed food industry began to grow in importance. Advances in technology were allowing processors to make new food products that were cheap but whose additives or ingredients were occasionally unhealthy or dangerous. For example, by the late nineteenth century, many food processors were making margarine from the by-products of slaughtered cattle and hogs and passing it off to the public as butter. Back then, margarine was made by combining animal fats with milk. The animal fats helped thicken the margarine, allowing processors to use less milk than is required to make butter. In this way, the cost of making the product decreased, but so too did its nutritional value.

While consumers objected to being deceived by the margarine producers, dairy farmers objected even more, since margarine, which was much cheaper than butter, threatened to cut into their sales. The public was also angry at food processors who were adulterating food with cheap thickeners that lowered their nutritional value. To adulterate food is to replace higher-quality ingredients with cheaper and lower-quality additives.

THE USDA AT WORK: RESEARCH AND EDUCATION

The Agricultural Research Service (ARS) is a scientific research agency within the USDA. The service provides those involved in the agricultural industry—including farmers—with the most up-to-date agricultural information to help solve farming problems (such as animal and plant pests and diseases), increase the size of farm crops and farmers' profits, and encourage environmentally friendly farming techniques.

One of the ARS's main tools in these efforts is the National Agricultural Library (NAL). The library was established as part of the USDA in 1862 by President Lincoln. It is the largest agricultural library in the world, with a collection of more than 3.3 million items and 48 miles (77 kilometers) of bookshelves. The collection includes books, journals, reports, photographs, films, videotapes, maps, and historic materials from as far back as the sixteenth century. Tens of thousands of new items are added each year in the NAL's ongoing effort to serve as the chief agricultural information resource in the United States, one that will help improve the quality of the American food supply and the lives of American farmers.

To make matters worse, the conditions at processing plants were often dangerously unsanitary (unclean).

To deal with these problems, Congress passed laws that gave the USDA additional powers to regulate and inspect food processors. A separate agency called the Division of Chemistry was created within the USDA. Its purpose was to examine food for evidence of adulteration. The new laws passed by Congress changed the basic purpose of the USDA. Now the USDA's mission would be expanded to defend the interests of consumers as well as those of farmers. From now on, the USDA would not only do research and issue reports. It would also take an active role in regulating, inspecting, and ensuring the safety of America's food supply.

Joining the Cabinet

By the late nineteenth century, farmers were faced with a new set of problems. As players in an increasingly complex national economy, farmers had more to worry about than the weather. They were concerned about the cost of grinding their grain at mills and shipping their products by rail and boat to faraway markets. They worried about the cost of borrowing money from banks (which they often needed to do in order to buy land or machinery). They were also concerned with the ups and downs of the prices their products would fetch and the profits they would earn with the sale of their products. These were problems faced by all American farmers, so they began to see themselves as a group with common interests to promote. These interests were often in sharp conflict with the interests of other groups involved in the agricultural industry, such as banks and railroad owners.

Farmers knew that the railroads and the bankers had a powerful influence on government policy. Their great wealth and power forced politicians to pay attention to them. Farmers had no such power. It became clear to them that they would have to band together if they hoped to gain any influence over the government. To this end, they organized farmers' groups such as the Grange and the People's Party (also called the Populists). These groups put pressure on Congress to raise the Department of Agriculture to the cabinet level. If this came to pass, the head of the USDA would become one of the president's key advisers. In theory at least, farmers would have a greater voice in government.

In 1887, the House of Representatives and the Senate passed bills that created a Department of Agriculture and Labor. This department would look out for the interests of farmers ("agriculture") and also of workers in many other industries ("labor"). Farmers objected to having their interests lumped together with the interests of industrial workers, so they opposed the bill and it never came to a vote. Only two years later, however, in 1889, President Grover Cleveland signed a bill into law that at last established the cabinet-level Department of Agriculture (a separate Department of Labor was established in 1913).

Changing Times and Changing Responsibilities

In the twentieth century, the processing of farm products, such as beef and produce, became increasingly industrial, creating a range of new problems and dangers for the American food

USDA meat inspectors examine slaughtered hogs at the Swift & Company meatpacking house in Chicago. After a public outcry over dangerous and filthy conditions in slaughterhouses and meatpacking plants, the U.S. Congress passed the Meat Inspection Act of 1906, allowing USDA inspectors to examine and condemn any tainted meat.

supply and average consumers. As a result, the responsibilities of the Department of Agriculture continued to expand to meet the new challenges of a modern, mechanized world. For example, around the turn of the twentieth century, journalists and novelists known as muckrakers were busy exposing the unsanitary conditions common in the meatpacking industry. Horrifying descriptions like those in Upton Sinclair's best-selling fact-based novel *The Jungle*—with its vivid depictions of dead rats and animal waste being ground into sausage—ruined many readers' appetites and led many Americans to demand that the meat industry be better supervised. Sales of beef suffered, which in turn hurt American farmers and ranchers.

Congress answered this demand for greater regulation of the meat industry by instituting a series of reforms through the Meat Inspection Act (1906). The Meat Inspection Act gave the secretary of agriculture the power to order meat inspections and condemn any meat that its inspectors found to be unfit for human consumption. The new requirements also gave the Department of Agriculture the responsibility for teaching consumers how to prepare meat more safely in order to prevent illness.

Public support for government intervention in daily life grew stronger than ever in the 1930s, the time of the Great Depression, when millions of Americans were out of work. The Depression was seen as a national emergency that called for a strong, energetic response by the government. The Depression era was particularly hard on American farmers because the economic crisis was coupled with an ecological catastrophe. Because of many years of poor farming techniques, nutrient-rich topsoil in parts of the Great Plains was being exhausted and was literally blowing away, a situation made worse by an extended drought across the region. This large area was known as the Dust Bowl,

This farmhouse in the Coldwater district north of Dalhart, Texas, was surrounded by dust in 1938. As with many Depression-era farms throughout the agricultural heartland, high winds, drought, and poor farming techniques led to the loss of the farmer's rich topsoil.

due to the dry and windy conditions that were stripping the land of soil. Many farmers were forced to abandon their land and seek work elsewhere, often thousands of miles away.

The farming crisis of the Depression era resulted in a much larger role for the USDA in agricultural matters. From the Depression onward, the secretary of agriculture evolved into a very powerful, though controversial, position in government. The story of the USDA and its growth from a minor, underfunded government bureau into one of the most important cabinet offices can best be told by discussing some of the most notable secretaries of agriculture in the office's history.

CHAPTER TWO

The Secretaries of Agriculture

Norman J. Coleman was appointed commissioner of the Department of Agriculture by President Grover Cleveland in 1885. During his time in office, he was influential in causing the department to be raised to a cabinet-level office in 1889, after which he briefly served as the department's first secretary. Cleveland's successor, President Benjamin Harrison, appointed Jeremiah McLain Rusk to replace Coleman as the secretary of agriculture. Rusk, who was born in 1830, was a former farmer who had gone on to serve as a U.S. representative from Wisconsin and then governor of that state. Since then, more than twenty-five secretaries of agriculture have been appointed and have served in the president's cabinet. Let's take a closer look at some of them.

Henry Agard Wallace

Depression-era hardships made Americans desire drastic action from their government. As a result, Congress was unusually receptive to President Franklin Roosevelt's sweeping social and economic plan, called the New Deal, which called for heavy government spending and investment in programs designed to create jobs, fight poverty, and improve society. A cornerstone of the New Deal was aid to farmers and nursing American agriculture back to health. Roosevelt picked Henry Agard Wallace to be his USDA secretary in 1933, and he encouraged Wallace to take a series of vigorous actions to help American farmers. The ultimate effect of Wallace's and Roosevelt's actions during the 1930s was to remake the USDA into a much larger and more active agency.

As editor of the highly influential agricultural newspaper *Wallace's Farmer* before his appointment as secretary of agriculture, Henry Agard Wallace made a number of suggestions to combat the farm depression taking hold in the late 1920s. To begin with, he recommended that farmers take steps to mechanize their farms, that is, to use less animal labor and more machine power to improve their farms' efficiency. Most people would probably have agreed with Wallace on this point.

Wallace had another idea, however, with which many people did not agree. He believed that the government should take steps to influence the prices of farm goods by reducing production if necessary. Wallace argued that, in order to keep crop supplies and prices stable and at a level that would allow farmers to make a decent living, farmers should be paid to grow fewer crops.

Though it might seem odd to encourage and even pay farmers to grow less, Wallace's idea addressed a major problem faced by American farmers. Farm products, like all goods, are subject to the economic law of supply and demand. The more there is of a commodity, the lower the price for it will be. Each individual farmer naturally wants to have a bumper crop. If all farmers produce more than average in a given year, however, the price at which they can sell their products goes down, and they make less money. Strange as it may seem, a great harvest can be almost as disastrous for farmers as floods or droughts. Wallace believed that reducing surpluses—the supply beyond what is needed—would make it easier for farmers to make a living and would help prevent family farms from going out of business.

The idea of paying farmers to grow less was controversial in the 1920s, and it has been controversial ever since. To some people it seems like socialism—when the government rather than individuals and private companies controls the production and distribution of goods. To others, it seems like welfare for farmers—supporting individuals who choose to stay in an industry that will not allow them to support themselves. To many, paying farmers not to farm is just illogical. Indeed, only

Secretary of Agriculture Henry Agard Wallace addresses a group of Vermont and New Hampshire farmers in Hanover, New Hampshire, in 1937. The son of the seventh secretary of agriculture, Wallace became the eleventh secretary in 1933 and was closely associated with Franklin Roosevelt's New Deal policies.

an event as catastrophic as the Great Depression would have made the average American ever consider the idea.

Wallace's ideas about government control of farm production were what first caught the attention of President Roosevelt and led to his appointing Wallace to head the Department of Agriculture. Once in office, Wallace supported the Agricultural Adjustment Administration (AAA), a program that built upon many of his earlier ideas. The AAA was established in 1933 by Congress to reduce crop supplies and increase the variety of crops planted. Farmers would be penalized with taxes if they grew staple crops (such as wheat, cotton, and tobacco) that were already in good supply, while they were encouraged with payments to plant soil-building crops (such as beans and ryegrass).

For his bold ideas about government regulation of American agriculture and his role in keeping many farmers on their land during the nation's most serious economic and

THE USDA AT WORK: RURAL HOUSING SERVICE

The Rural Housing Service (RHS) is one of the USDA's Rural Development programs. It is charged with providing decent, safe, sanitary, and affordable housing and community facilities to rural areas. The RHS helps pay for new or improved housing for 60,000 moderate-, low-, and very low-income families. In addition, it helps pay for the construction or improvement of firehouses, day care centers, libraries, hospitals, and other essential community facilities. The RHS also provides loans to rural families to help them buy, build, or repair their homes, and it subsidizes (helps pay) rent for those who do not own their own homes. Because farm workers are among the most poorly housed and lowest paid of American workers, the USDA provides loans to farm owners to build housing for the laborers they employ.

agricultural crisis, Wallace is still considered the most important secretary of agriculture in American history.

Ezra Taft Benson

During the 1940s, Presidents Franklin Roosevelt and Harry Truman, both Democrats, appointed agriculture secretaries who continued Wallace's activist programs. By the end of the decade, though, public support for big government began to decline as the nation emerged from the Depression and World War II (1939–1945) and began to enjoy an economic boom. When Republican president Dwight D. Eisenhower assumed office in 1953, he appointed Ezra Taft Benson to the post of secretary of agriculture.

Benson, who came from Utah, was one of the most conservative secretaries of agriculture in the history of the office. As secretary of agriculture, his major goal was to reduce the role that government played in the business of farming.

Benson served for both of Eisenhower's terms, from 1953 to 1961, during which he worked hard to get rid of price supports and production controls. He believed these harmed the American character by inspiring laziness and a dependency on "handouts." Representatives from farm states, however, remained unconvinced and were unwilling to anger farmers by siding with Benson. In the end, Benson could not muster enough support in his own party to reduce price supports, and they remained in place.

Benson's task was especially hard because when he took office in the early 1950s, advances in technology were making U.S. farming more productive than ever. New equipment allowed farmers to work more land, while scientific advances were helping to increase the size and health of crops. As a result, farm surpluses were going up, and thanks to the law of supply and demand, farm prices were going down. This was the very situation price supports and production controls were supposed to prevent. The main alternative to price controls seemed to be to let crop prices plummet and farmers across the country go out of business. Benson found little support in Congress or among American voters for this plan of action. By the decade's end, therefore, government subsidies to farmers, instead of going down, had greatly increased.

Orville Freeman

In 1960, Americans elected a Democrat, John F. Kennedy, to be their president. By this time, the USDA was considered to be such a controversial office that the post of secretary of agriculture was called the "hot seat." Soon after Kennedy was elected president, he appointed Orville Freeman to fill that hot seat. Freeman accepted the offer and held the job for eight years under Presidents Kennedy and Lyndon B. Johnson.

When Freeman took office as secretary of agriculture, American farmers were still producing more food than they could sell, creating large surpluses. Unlike Benson, Freeman had no qualms about paying farmers to decrease their production.

Another more innovative and productive way that Freeman dealt with the problems that surpluses were creating for farmers was to distribute the surplus food to poor people who would otherwise have gone hungry and to sell it abroad. In 1963, at the height of Cold War tensions between the United States and

Grain is being prepared for shipment from Charleston, South Carolina, to Russia. Following the collapse of Communism in the former Soviet Union and Russia's resulting struggle to create a capitalist democracy, the U.S. government began a $1 billion aid program to assist its former enemy. As part of this program, the USDA shipped tons of food to Russia.

the Soviet Union, the USDA made the first of many agreements to sell wheat to the Soviets, who were experiencing shortages of grain.

Though Freeman had considered production controls necessary, he was never really happy with them. In speeches he made in later years, Freeman spoke of the need to solve the riddle of modern agriculture—how can so many people be starving in a world full of food? Freeman was highly critical of American agriculture's reluctance to find workable solutions to this problem.

New Challenges for Today's Agriculture Secretaries

While prices and production controls continue to be controversial matters, the years have brought new concerns for the USDA. These include the effects of modern farming methods on the environment, on human health, and on the well-being of animals. The value of organic farming (farming that does not use pesticides and chemical fertilizers) is another new area of interest. The possible dangers posed by genetically modified crops (the use of high-tech scientific techniques to create breeds of plants never before seen on this planet) are a growing concern. These problems generate strong feelings in many people, both within the agricultural industry and among consumers.

The secretary of agriculture must be able to balance three things: ensuring that family farmers remain on their land and farm it efficiently, satisfying the desire for profit among larger agribusiness farms, and fulfilling the needs of consumers for an affordable, plentiful, and safe food supply. Meeting all three of these goals is an extremely challenging task, which is why the secretary of the Department of Agriculture remains in the hot seat.

CHAPTER THREE

How the USDA Works

The secretary of agriculture is in charge of one of the biggest departments in the federal government. The USDA is responsible for many different programs, including agricultural research; food aid to poor people and school-age children; the promotion of land, water, and soil conservation; and the administration of national forests and grasslands. The USDA makes it possible for farmers to take out loans that help pay for the running of their farms. The department helps rural areas receive telephone, electric, water, and sewer services. It also tries to make sure that the food delivered to consumers' tables is safe to eat. In order to ensure food safety, the USDA inspects meat, dairy, and poultry products. When

farm animals are suspected of having a disease, the USDA organizes quarantines to keep the disease from spreading. A quarantine involves the removal of a sick animal from the rest of the herd to prevent spread of the disease.

Today, the USDA has twenty major operating units—each of which is a government agency in itself, with a large budget and thousands of employees. The USDA's operating units fall into seven basic mission areas. These are:

- Farm and Agricultural Service
- Food, Nutrition, and Consumer Services
- Food Safety and Inspection Service
- Natural Resources and Environment
- Research, Education, and Economics
- Marketing and Regulatory Programs
- Rural Development

Farm and Agricultural Service

Throughout history, farmers have been at the mercy of nature. Droughts, floods, plant diseases, plagues of locusts or other insect pests—these are just a few examples of the kinds of natural disasters that can destroy crops. The USDA's Farm and Agricultural Service (FAS) reduces the risks of farming by helping farmers with the business and financial aspects of agriculture. For example, its Farm Service Agency (FSA) gives loans to farmers who are having trouble getting loans from private banks. Often FSA borrowers are new farmers who do not yet have enough assets—such as land, a house, farm equipment—to qualify for conventional loans. The agency helps keep afloat established farmers who have suffered financial setbacks due to natural disasters, bad weather, and crop failures, through both crop insurance and disaster relief. The agency also makes special payments to farmers who plant crops such as buckwheat, ryegrass, clover, and barley, which improve poor land and prevent soil erosion.

Another agency, the Foreign Agricultural Service (FAS), gives American farmers assistance and support in exporting, or sending, their products overseas. For example, the FAS helps farmers research foreign markets and find buyers for American farm products. The FAS also gives farmers the opportunity to participate in programs that distribute food in developing nations.

Food, Nutrition, and Consumer Services

Ever since the 1930s, the USDA has distributed some of the nation's food surplus to poor people, to help make sure that nobody in the United States goes hungry. The USDA distributes surplus food through programs such as Food, Nutrition, and Consumer Services, which enables low-income families to buy food by giving them food stamp coupons, and the Child

33

THE USDA AT WORK: CHILDHOOD NUTRITION

Not only does the USDA help farmers produce the food that America eats, it also helps provide that food to those most in need. One of the most important food and nutrition programs in which the USDA participates is the National School Lunch Program. Every school day, in almost 97,000 schools and day care facilities throughout the nation, 27 million children are served well-balanced, low-cost or free lunches and after-school snacks. Every school that takes part in the program receives cash and food from the USDA to help provide the meals. To ensure that school meals are nutritious, in 1994 the USDA began the School Meals Initiative for Healthy Children. This program makes sure that school food meets USDA dietary guidelines. It also educates children about good nutrition and trains school kitchen staffs in safe food preparation and storage and the creation of healthy menus.

School workers prepare USDA peaches for the school lunch program at T. C. Williams High School in Alexandria, Virginia.

An inspector for the USDA's Food Safety and Inspection Service (FSIS) examines chickens on a poultry processing line. The FSIS protects public health by regulating meat, poultry, and egg products. This includes all raw beef, pork, lamb, chicken, and turkey, as well as processed meat and poultry products, including hams, sausages, soups, stews, pizzas, and frozen dinners.

Nutrition programs, which are responsible for the low price of meals at public schools. Food, Nutrition, and Consumer Services also supports programs that educate children and adults about good nutrition.

Food Safety and Inspection Service

The USDA is responsible for making sure that the nation's supply of meat, poultry, dairy, and egg products are safe, wholesome, and accurately labeled and packaged. The mission of food safety is carried out by just one operating agency, the Food Safety and Inspection Service (FSIS). Contaminated food can kill people, so the job of this operating agency is, quite simply, a matter of life and death.

The FSIS also tries to teach people how to store and prepare food safely at home. To this end, it publishes books and pamphlets about food safety, conducts public service advertising campaigns, and maintains a Meat and Poultry Hotline that people can call when they have questions about safe storage, handling, and preparation of food.

Natural Resources and Environment

Farmers have always known that in order for land to remain productive, it has to be carefully managed. In the early years of the United States, however, there was so much land in comparison to the amount of people who were available to work it that not much attention was paid to protecting the land and keeping it fertile. Nor was much thought given to preserving the great forests that blanketed much of the American continent. No one could imagine then that the country would become so heavily settled and populated that the land and forests would someday be endangered.

Since that time, we have learned the hard way—particularly during the Dust Bowl of the 1920s and 1930s, when drought and erosion turned vast areas of the Great Plains into a wasteland— that good land management means thinking beyond immediate financial gain and planning for the future health and long-term profitability of farmlands and forests. Today, most Americans

Because America's forests are considered an important agricultural resource, the USDA is charged with protecting them through its Forest Service. Fighting wildfires every year is one of the Forest Service's main responsibilities. In 2002, there were 88,458 fires, burning a total of almost 7 million acres (2.8 million hectares).

agree that it is necessary to protect and manage the environment carefully if it is going to be here for future generations to enjoy.

The USDA shares with other agencies—such as the Environmental Protection Agency (EPA) and the Department of the Interior—the responsibility for maintaining America's natural resources. Within the USDA, the Forest Service manages America's wilderness areas and works with other agencies to prevent and combat fires. The USDA's Natural Resources Conservation Service (NRCS) gives farmers the latest information on environmentally friendly farming practices, such as reduced use of chemical fertilizers and pesticides (which can pollute the water supply) and organic methods that can be used to replace them.

Research, Education, and Economics

Collecting and distributing information about farming practices was the first major responsibility of the USDA in the mid-nineteenth century. Today, the Department of Agriculture continues to keep farmers informed about the latest advances in farming techniques, explanations of the newest equipment, important new trends, studies on the economic health of the industry and its farmers, and weather and crop reports and forecasts.

Marketing and Regulatory Programs

Farming today is big business, both at home and abroad. American agricultural products are sold throughout the United States and all around the world. The USDA's marketing and regulatory programs are designed to help American farmers compete with other nations' growers in worldwide trade. The same programs also help farmers and consumers address some of the negative consequences of world trade, such as accidental importation of plant or animal diseases. When a plant, animal, or virus comes into an environment where it has never been before, it can spread very quickly, upsetting the balance of nature. Today, invasive species, which include many insect pests, are a major problem in the United States and around the world. The USDA helps guard against the appearance of foreign pests and plant and animal viruses in the United States and helps in the fight against those that are imported.

Rural Development

The USDA is not only concerned with the work that is done on American farms, but it is also committed to improving the larger communities in which farmers live and work. Healthy and vibrant rural communities help to foster productive farms and successful farmers. Farmers have almost always lived far from cities, many miles away from the densely populated areas where modern technology and the comforts and benefits it brings tend to appear first. Many rural areas were without electricity, indoor plumbing, and telephone service well into the 1930s and 1940s. During the Depression, Secretary of Agriculture Henry Agard Wallace made bringing these modern services to rural areas the responsibility of the USDA.

Although the condition of rural America has changed dramatically since then, many of its needs are still unmet. It often lags behind the rest of the country in terms of local services and modern conveniences. The USDA continues to develop programs to bring good housing, water, and energy systems to rural communities. Just as rich soil is necessary to produce healthy crops, a thriving community will help nurture successful farms.

CHAPTER FOUR

The USDA in the Twenty-first Century

Agriculture has changed a great deal since Abraham Lincoln's time, when the USDA was founded. Gas-powered tractors, plows, and harvesters have replaced horses, oxen, and laborers, while small family farms, which were once the norm, have become more and more overshadowed by huge corporate growers. The only real certainty in agriculture today is that the industry will continue to change. Twenty-first-century farming practices and equipment will almost certainly seem strange and primitive to twenty-second-century Americans. The USDA now faces challenges and opportunities that could not have been imagined 200 years ago. This chapter will discuss a few of the most important new developments confronting modern

secretaries of agriculture. Their responses to changes in the industry will affect the fortunes of tomorrow's farmers and determine the future of American agriculture.

Genetically Modified Agricultural Products

Genetically modified agricultural products are new breeds of plants and animals that have been created by the latest laboratory methods. Scientists today can create new kinds of plants and animals by taking genes from one species and adding them to another. These modern genetic techniques can create breeds of animals and plants that are resistant to disease or pests, grow bigger or more quickly, taste better, are more nutritious, and have a longer shelf life. Genetically modified plants and animals can even be used to create products other than food, including medicines, vaccines, organs for transplant, and plastics.

Genetically modified plants and animals are already a part of American agriculture, but not everyone considers them a good idea. Why these foods should be controversial may not be obvious at first glance. When the possibility of genetically modified foods was first discussed, the future they offered seemed promising. Farmers would be able to grow wheat that bugs could not eat, eliminating the need for toxic pesticides. They would be able to grow crops that would be more nutritious, more suited to harsh environments, more resistant to disease, and faster growing. This would offer new hope for many third world countries that had long experienced drought, food shortages, and starvation.

41

Demonstrators wave signs that express their opposition to genetically modified foods during a protest in Chicago on November 18, 1999. The Food and Drug Administration, a government agency charged with ensuring the safety and quality of America's food supply and medicines, was holding its first public meeting on the safety of genetically modified foods.

Many consumers, scientists, and politicians fear the unknown consequences of introducing genetically modified plants and animals into the food chain, however. Just because genetically modified plants are confined in a separate field does not mean their genetic changes will not get accidentally introduced to the wider world. Because many plants reproduce through pollen, which can be carried many miles on the wind, a normal plant may be fertilized by a genetically modified plant from a field miles away. Unplanned mutations could occur, and genetically modified material could enter the food chain without anyone's knowledge.

Some worry that people will develop allergies to new substances in food or that a plant's new genetic resistance to pests or herbicides will be passed on to wild plants, creating hardy weeds that cannot be contained or killed. Others wonder how far the genetic changes will reach into the food chain. What, for example, will the effects be on a baby whose breast milk comes from a mother who ate the meat of a pig that was fed on corn genetically modified to be toxic to pests?

The modern agricultural industry produces the abundance we see in our farm stands, supermarkets, and restaurants. This agricultural wealth has been made possible by many important, though controversial, innovations that farmers have introduced in the past. These innovations carried great risks and a heavy price— the change from horse and mule farming to factory farming drove millions of people off the land. The use of fertilizers and pesticides continues to alarm environmentalists, even as the size of crops has increased to help feed more of the earth's people.

Without modern agricultural techniques, there would not be enough food to support the world's current population. Without further innovations, we will not be able to feed the even larger population that will inhabit the earth in the near future. It is the USDA's job to carefully study the issue of genetically modified foods and draw up guidelines and regulations that will balance the needs of farmers, agricultural scientists, food processors, American consumers, and the hungry world beyond our borders. Above all, the USDA must put considerations of health and safety above those of profit.

THE USDA AT WORK: PROTECTING THE CONSUMER

The Food Safety and Inspection Service (FSIS) is the agency within the USDA that is responsible for ensuring the safety, wholesomeness, and correct labeling and packaging of meat, poultry, and egg products. The FSIS sets standards for food safety and inspects all raw and processed meat and poultry products and egg products sold in the United States, including imported foods. The FSIS also examines animals before and after they are killed in order to prevent diseased meat from entering the food supply.

These two dogs are part of the USDA's Beagle Brigade—a group of detector dogs that sniff travelers' luggage for prohibited fruits, plants, and meat.

The FSIS has been doing this good work for more than a century. At the dawn of the twenty-first century, however, the service is confronting new dangers to our food supply— terrorism and biosecurity threats. Today, many government officials and ordinary citizens are worried that terrorists could try to harm Americans by contaminating the food supply with deadly toxins or poisons. In cooperation with the Department of Homeland Security, the Centers for Disease Control and Prevention, the Food and Drug Administration, and the Environmental Protection Agency, the FSIS is working harder than ever to protect the food Americans eat by identifying any possible biosecurity threats and preventing them before they have a chance to be carried out.

Chemical Vs. Organic Farming

One of the greatest problems farmers have had to contend with throughout human history has been the destruction of their crops by insects. Insects have destroyed entire crops and caused famines (periods when large numbers of people starve from lack of food). While famine has rarely been a problem in the United States, insects have often taken a serious toll on crops and on the people whose livelihood depends upon them.

The twentieth century's solution to the insect problem was the use of pesticides—poisons sprayed on plants that killed insects but were thought to be harmless to human beings. The use of pesticides transformed agriculture in America and around the world. The high productivity of American farmers and the beautiful, spotless fruit and vegetables we see in our grocery stores are a direct result of farming with pesticides.

With the publication of *Silent Spring* in 1962, Rachel Carson *(center)* warned about the dangers to human health and the environment of pesticides, like those being sprayed by a plane over a California field at left. Many farmers now seek natural alternatives, such as the ladybugs at right, which eat certain pests that plague American crops.

There is just one problem, however. It turns out that many pesticides are, in fact, harmful to human beings, as well as to other animals and plants. Even when pesticides do not go directly into our bodies when we eat treated food, they can be washed off of leaves and into the ground by rain. They can then enter the soil and water supply, where they add to the buildup of toxic chemicals in our environment. Chemical fertilizers, too, can seep into and contaminate the water supply. The amount of illness and death they cause is unknown. Some people attribute the high rates of cancer in developed countries partly to the use of pesticides and fertilizers.

One solution to American farmers' dependence on pesticides and fertilizers is organic farming—farming that uses a variety of natural, nontoxic techniques to limit insect damage without using pesticides. Regular crop rotation (the planting of different crops on a certain field) and occasionally allowing fields to remain fallow (unplanted) for a short time help keep soil naturally rich in nutrients.

Organic farming does not only benefit human health. Animals on organic farms enjoy much more humane living conditions than do animals on conventional farms. For example, they are often allowed to roam freely rather than stay confined in small and overcrowded pens. They are not overfed in order to gain weight quickly. They are also not given hormones that will make them produce more milk or grow larger. Despite the benefits of organic farming to humans and animals alike, however, only about 2 percent of the U.S. food supply is grown organically.

The problem is that organic farming is much more expensive than regular farming. This makes a big difference to consumers, as is clear to anyone who has compared the food prices at a health food store with those at an ordinary supermarket. Organic farming usually requires more land and more labor, and that translates into higher prices at the checkout counter.

Those in favor of regular farming methods argue that the health benefits of providing nutritious food at a price everybody can afford outweigh the health risks posed by pesticides, genetic modification, and other high-tech farming techniques. Organic farmers counter this argument by saying that safe food and healthy families are worth a few extra dollars at the supermarket checkout. In addition, they claim that cleaning up the pollution related to chemical farming techniques and treating diseases that may have environmental causes costs the American economy far more than the additional expenses of organic farming.

The USDA's challenge as it heads into the twenty-first century will be to encourage greater adoption of organic farming methods while also seeking to identify and develop safer high-tech aids to farmers seeking to fight pests and diseases and increase their crop size. If it can find ways to bring down the price of organic farming while also boosting the environmental safety of conventional farming, the gap between organic and conventional farmers will be narrowed and divisions lessened. And American agriculture will grow stronger than ever.

Subsidies, Tariffs, and Free Trade

The products of American farmers are sold all around the world. Americans, in turn, buy lots of food from outside the United States. Farming today is an international business. This means that farmers in different countries are in direct competition with one another. What farmers do in other countries affects American farmers, just as American farm practices influence other countries' agricultural industries.

For example, if the cost of producing grain is lower in the United States than in France, American farmers will be able to sell grain at a lower price than French farmers and still make a profit. Since people everywhere prefer to buy their grain at the lowest available price, French farmers will have to sell their grain at the same low price, even if that means they will not make a profit. If this goes on year after year, the French farmers will be driven out of business.

How could the French government help its farmers to survive in the face of U.S. competition? First, the French government could put a type of tax called a tariff on American grain imported into France, making it more expensive for French consumers. This way, the French farmers could at least be sure of selling their grain in their own country. Or, instead of a tariff (or in addition to it), the French government could pay money to French farmers, thereby lowering their production costs and making their grain price competitive with the Americans'. Payments like these are called subsidies.

Rich countries tend to support their farmers with subsidies. Poor countries tend to support their farmers by taxing imports because they do not have enough money available to pay subsidies. Economists say that tariffs are bad policy. The trouble with taxing imports is that it discourages trade. This damages the world economy. Economists call tariffs trade barriers and argue instead for its opposite: free trade. Free trade encourages producers in each country to provide quality goods at reasonable prices. If they produce sloppy or overpriced goods, they will find few buyers. This worldwide competition is thought to make companies and industries more efficient and the world as a whole more wealthy. Not everyone agrees, however, that free trade is good for the entire world.

Most of the world's wealthiest and most developed countries are supporters of free trade, claiming it creates greater fairness and opportunity for all the world's nations. To the farmers of the world's poorest countries, however, free trade is anything but fair. Generally, only rich countries are able to subsidize their farmers. So subsidies give the farmers of rich countries an unfair advantage in world trade by allowing them to sell their goods for less. The amount countries spend on farm subsidies amounts to about $1 billion a day. With the help of subsidies, farmers of the developed world undersell farmers in African nations and India who live in desperate poverty, unaided by their governments.

Advocates for developing nations insist that subsidies are really just trade barriers in disguise and that subsidies help protect the products of wealthy nations from competing directly with those of the third world. Eliminating these subsidies, however, would mean making American farmers pay to solve the problems of poverty in other countries. It is hard to imagine a U.S. secretary of agriculture, or a U.S. president, of either the Democratic or Republican Party, who could rally public support for a move like that. Yet this problem is very real, and it is just one of the many complex issues that will face future secretaries of agriculture.

Conclusion

Once America was a primarily agricultural country, with 75 to 90 percent of its citizens involved in farming. Now, America is a highly industrialized country, and only around 3 percent of the U.S. population earns its living from the land. Amazingly, however, that 3 percent grows more than enough to feed the nation's 250 million people and export a giant surplus every year. Within the space of a hundred years, Americans have gone from growing and harvesting by mules, horses, and humans to a far more mechanized and industrial style of farming. They harvest with giant combines—machines that cut the wheat, thresh it, bag it, and bale the hay in a single operation. They keep livestock healthy with antibiotics and encourage them

Agricultural engineer Kenneth Sudduth examines a sample of grain collected from his combine's grain flow sensor. The flow sensor is a high-tech instrument that helps farmers measure the amount of grain being harvested by the combine. Other sensors allow farmers to measure the moisture content of the grain (allowing them to estimate drying costs) and estimate the extent of the harvested area.

to produce more milk with the help of synthetic (human-made) hormones. Americans have even begun cloning barn animals and creating better, stronger crops through genetic engineering.

Though many of the changes in the agricultural industry are the result of technological advances, the future of farming must not be determined only by scientists and agribusiness executives. As it has done for almost 150 years during periods of great and bewildering change, the USDA must continue to ensure that the food supply remains safe and plentiful. It must guarantee that the American consumer has access to a nutritious, balanced, and affordable diet. It must also make sure that the environment is not sacrificed to considerations of quick profit. Above all, the USDA must continue to protect the livelihoods of rural communities and their family farmers while also seeing to it that the nation—and the world beyond—does not go hungry.

TIMELINE

1776	George Washington suggests to the Continental Congress the establishment of a national Board of Agriculture.
1860	Farmers make up 58 percent of the American workforce.
1862	The USDA is created. The first USDA research bulletin is issued.
1863	The first monthly crop report is published by the USDA.
1868	The USDA begins research on animal diseases.
1870	Forty-seven percent of employed Americans work in agriculture. This is the first time in the nation's history that farmers form a minority of the U.S. workforce.
1873	The Washington navel orange is introduced into California by the USDA.
1874	Oleomargarine is first manufactured in the United States.
1880	Forty-nine percent of Americans are employed in agriculture. One out of every four farmers is a tenant farmer (who rents the land he or she farms from a landowner). Evaporated milk is first developed.
1883	Methods are developed to detect food adulteration.
1889	The Department of Agriculture is given cabinet status.
February 15, 1889–March 6, 1889	**Norman Jay Coleman**
March 6, 1889–March 6, 1893	**Jeremiah McLain Rusk**

| 1890 | The Meat Inspection Acts are passed, authorizing inspection of pork, bacon, and live animals intended for export and the quarantine of animals being imported. |

| March 7, 1893–March 5, 1897 | Julius Sterling Morton |

| March 6, 1897–March 5, 1913 | James Wilson |

| 1899 | The USDA begins the field mapping of soils. |

| 1900 | Thirty-eight percent of employed Americans work in agriculture. |

| 1906 | The Pure Food and Drug Act and the 1906 Meat Inspection Act are passed. |

| 1912 | The Federal Plant Quarantine Act is passed. The Seed Importation Act forbids entry into the United States of certain adulterated grains and seeds unfit for seeding purposes. |

| March 6, 1913–February 2, 1920 | David Franklin Houston |

| 1916 | The Federal Farm Loan Act is passed. |

| 1917 | The first official grade standard for fruits and vegetables is issued by the USDA when it sets standards for potatoes. |

| 1920 | A soil classification system is developed. |

| February 2, 1920–March 4, 1921 | Edwin Thomas Meredith |

| March 5, 1921–October 25, 1924 | Henry Cantwell Wallace |

| November 22, 1924–March 4, 1925 | Howard Mason Gore |

| March 5, 1925–March 4, 1929 | William Marion Jardine |

| 1926 | The USDA begins inspections of live poultry. |

| 1928 | The USDA begins research on soil erosion and its effects on agricultural productivity. |

| March 6, 1929–March 4, 1933 | Arthur Mastick Hyde |

| 1933 | The Farm Credit Administration is established. The Soil Erosion Service is established (later renamed the Natural Resources Conservation Service). The Agricultural Adjustment Act puts crop controls in place. |

| March 4, 1933–September 4, 1940 | Henry Agard Wallace |

| 1934 | The worst drought in U.S. history takes hold in the Great Plains and covers more than 75 percent of the country. |

| 1939 | The Federal Seed Act is passed, requiring truthful labeling of seeds and forbidding the importation of low-quality seeds. The USDA issues the first grade standards for a frozen product—peas. |

| September 5, 1940–June 29, 1945 | Claude Raymond Wickard |

| 1941 | The USDA publishes its first daily nutrition guide. |

| 1943 | The USDA begins researching the creation of fruit essences that will lead to the development of concentrated frozen juices. |

| June 30, 1945–May 10, 1948 | Clinton Presba Anderson |

| 1946 | The National School Lunch Act is passed. High-quality frozen orange juice concentrate is first developed. |

| June 2, 1948–January 20, 1953 | Charles Franklin Brannan |

| 1950 | Eleven percent of working Americans are employed in agriculture. |

| January 21, 1953–January 20, 1961 | Ezra Taft Benson |

| 1957 | The Humane Slaughter Act, the Poultry Inspection Act, and the Federal Plant Pest Act are passed. |

| January 21, 1961–January 20, 1969 | Orville Lothrop Freeman |

| 1967 | The Wholesome Meat Act is passed. |

| 1968 | The Wholesome Poultry Products Act is passed. |

| 1969 | The Food and Nutrition Service is established. |

January 21, 1969–November 17, 1971 | Clifford Morris Hardin

1970 | Farmers make up less than 5 percent of the U.S. workforce. The Environmental Protection Agency is established. The Wheat Research and Promotion Act and the Egg Products Inspection Act are passed.

1971 | The Animal and Plant Health Inspection Service is established and is responsible for regulatory and control programs relating to animal and plant diseases and pests.

December 2, 1971–October 4, 1976 | Earl Lauer Butz

November 4, 1976–January 20, 1977 | John Albert Knebel

January 23, 1977–January 20, 1981 | Bob Bergland

January 23, 1981–February 14, 1986 | John Rusling Block

March 7, 1986–January 21, 1989 | Richard Edmund Lyng

February 16, 1989–March 1, 1991 | Clayton Yeutter

1990 | The Food, Agriculture, Conservation, and Trade Act is passed.

March 12, 1991–January 20, 1993 | Edward Rell Madigan

January 22, 1993–December 31, 1994 | Mike Espy

March 30, 1995–January 19, 2001 | Daniel Robert Glickman

2000 | The Food Safety Initiative is passed, authorizing food safety inspections to decrease foodborne illnesses.

January 20, 2001–January 20, 2005 | Ann M. Veneman

2001 | Secretary Veneman releases "Agricultural Policy: Taking Stock for the New Century." This policy document outlined emerging trends in agriculture, including trade expansion, conservation and the environment, rural communities, and nutrition.

January 21, 2005 | Mike Johanns

GLOSSARY

agribusiness An industry that is involved in day-to-day farm operations; the manufacture, sale, and delivery of farm equipment and supplies; and the processing, storage, sale, and delivery of farm commodities, like crops, dairy products, and livestock.

agriculture The science, art, or practice of cultivating the soil, producing crops, raising livestock, and selling farm products.

cabinet A council of the chief advisers of a head of state.

catastrophe A tragic event or violent natural disaster.

commodity A good that can be bought and sold.

cultivation The preparation of soil for the raising of crops.

export To send something outside of one's country.

federal Relating to the central governing authority in a nation made up of several states or territories.

genes The basic units of the nucleic acids DNA and RNA (which are the building blocks of all plant and animal life) that control the traits and characteristics handed down from generation to generation within a family of living things.

import To bring into one's country something from another country.

intervention The entering into a situation in order to affect or change its outcome.

organic Relating to the use of food produced without chemical fertilizers, growth stimulants, antibiotics, or pesticides.

surplus The amount of something that remains after the need for it is satisfied.

tariff An extra tax or charge placed upon imported (and sometimes exported) goods.

toxic Poisonous.

unsanitary Unclean or unhealthy.

FOR MORE INFORMATION

Farm Service Agency (FSA)
1400 Independence Ave. SW
STOP 0506
Washington, DC 20250
Web site: http://www.fsa.usda.gov

Food Safety and Inspection Service
United States Department
   of Agriculture
Washington, DC 20250
(202) 720-9113
Web site: http://www.fsis.usda.gov

Natural Resources
   Conservation Service
Conservation Communications Staff
P.O. Box 2890
Washington, DC 20013
Web site: http://www.nrcs.usda.gov

USDA Food and Nutrition Service
3101 Park Center Dr., Room 926

Alexandria, VA 22302
Web site: http://www.fns.usda.
   gov/fns

USDA Forest Service
P.O. Box 96090
Washington, DC 20090
(202) 205-8333
Web site: http://www.fs.fed.us

WEB SITES
Due to the changing nature of
Internet links, the Rosen Publishing
Group, Inc., has developed an
online list of Web sites related to
the subject of this book. This site is
updated regularly. Please use this
link to access the list:

www.rosenlinks.com/tyg/agri

FOR FURTHER READING

Feinberg, Barbara Silberdick. *The Cabinet*. Breckenridge, CO: Twenty-first Century Books, 1997.

Hansen, Ann Larkin. *All Kinds of Farms*. Edina, MN: Checkerboard Library, 1998.

Horn, Geoffrey M. *The Cabinet and Federal Agencies*. New York, NY: World Almanac, 2003.

Keen, Jared, ed. *The Future of Farming*. Calgary, Alberta, Canada: Weigl Educational Associates, 2003.

Marshall, Elizabeth L. *Hi-Tech Harvest: A Look at Genetically Engineered Foods*. New York, NY: Franklin Watts, 1999.

Wellman, Sam. *The Cabinet*. Broomall, PA: Chelsea House Publishers, 2001.

Wilkes, Angela. *A Farm Through Time*. New York, NY: DK Publishing, 2001.

BIBLIOGRAPHY

"Agencies, Services, and Programs." USDA.gov. 1997. Retrieved October 2003 (http://www.usda.gov/services.html).

Charles, Daniel. *Lords of the Harvest: Biotech, Big Money, and the Future of Food.* New York, NY: The Perseus Books Group, 2001.

"Chronological History by Decade from the Creation of the USDA in 1862 until 2000." Agricultural Research Service. 2002. Retrieved December 2003 (http://www.ars.usda.gov/is/timeline/chron.htm).

Gardner, Bruce L. *American Agriculture in the Twentieth Century: How It Flourished and What It Cost.* Cambridge, MA: Harvard University Press, 2002.

Hurt, R. Douglas. *American Agriculture: A Brief History.* Ames, IA: Iowa State University Press, 1994.

Hurt, R. Douglas. *Problems of Plenty: The American Farmer in the Twentieth Century.* Chicago, IL: Ivan R. Dee, Inc., 2002.

Lurguin, Paul F. *High Tech Harvest: Understanding Genetically Modified Food Plants.* Boulder, CO: Westview Press, 2002.

"The People's Department." USDA.gov. 1997. Retrieved October 2003 (http://www.usda.gov/yourusda/layout.htm).

"Secretaries of Agriculture." USDA.gov. 2001. Retrieved October 2003 (http://www.usda.gov/history/pastsec.htm).

INDEX